"In the English language area it has been relatively quiet around Thomas à Kempis for a long time. If any good studies appeared, they often passed the general public by. In this book Greg Peters makes a courageous and much needed attempt to bring the meaning of this influential spiritual writer back to the attention of the public. It contains good and surprising insights into both the life and work of a man who, because of his familiarity with Christ through Scripture and his great psychological empathy, still reaches many readers today."

—P. (Paul) J. J. van Geest
Tilburg University, Erasmus University Rotterdam, KU Leuven

"Who purifies the heart makes room inwardly for God. The more we work on our interior, the less individualistic we become and the more we grow in communion with each other. This is the message of Thomas à Kempis's *Imitation of Christ*, beautifully explained by Greg Peters to be a book that belongs to its own age but is still relevant today."

—Charles Caspers
Titus Brandsma Institute, Nijmegen

"This book is a well-written introduction in the spiritual theology of Thomas à Kempis, the writer of the famous *Imitation of Christ*. It gives access to the richness of this unique source of life. Everyone living in this challenging world and desiring to follow Jesus Christ devoutedly may drink from this well. Simplicity and depth are the entrances into this treasure of Christian mysticism."

—Kees Waaijman
Titus Brandsma Institute, Nijmegen

THOMAS À KEMPIS

CASCADE COMPANIONS

The Christian theological tradition provides an embarrassment of riches: from Scripture to modern scholarship, we are blessed with a vast and complex theological inheritance. And yet this feast of traditional riches is too frequently inaccessible to the general reader.

The Cascade Companions series addresses the challenge by publishing books that combine academic rigor with broad appeal and readability. They aim to introduce nonspecialist readers to that vital storehouse of authors, documents, themes, histories, arguments, and movements that comprise this heritage with brief yet compelling volumes.

RECENT TITLES IN THIS SERIES:

Feminism and Christianity by Caryn D. Griswold
Angels, Worms, and Bogeys by Michelle A. Clifton-Soderstrom
Christianity and Politics by C. C. Pecknold
A Way to Scholasticism by Peter S. Dillard
Theological Theodicy by Daniel Castelo
The Letter to the Hebrews in Social-Scientific Perspective
    by David A. deSilva
Basil of Caesarea by Andrew Radde-Galwitz
A Guide to St. Symeon the New Theologian by Hannah Hunt
Reading John by Christopher W. Skinner
Forgiveness by Anthony Bash
Jacob Arminius by Rustin Brian
The Rule of Faith: A Guide by Everett Ferguson
Jeremiah: Prophet Like Moses by Jack Lundbom
Richard Hooker: A Companion to His Life and Work by W. Bradford
    Littlejohn
Scripture's Knowing: A Companion to Biblical Epistemology by Dru
    Johnson
John Calvin by Donald McKim
Rudolf Bultmann: A Companion to His Theology by David Congdon
The U.S. Immigration Crisis: Toward an Ethics of Place
    by Miguel A. De La Torre

THOMAS À KEMPIS

His Life and Spiritual Theology

GREG PETERS

CASCADE *Books* · Eugene, Oregon

THOMAS À KEMPIS
His Life and Spiritual Theology

Cascade Companions

Copyright © 2021 Greg Peters. All rights reserved. Except for brief quotations in critical publications or reviews, no part of this book may be reproduced in any manner without prior written permission from the publisher. Write: Permissions, Wipf and Stock Publishers, 199 W. 8th Ave., Suite 3, Eugene, OR 97401.

Cascade Books
An Imprint of Wipf and Stock Publishers
199 W. 8th Ave., Suite 3
Eugene, OR 97401

www.wipfandstock.com

PAPERBACK ISBN: 978-1-5326-5706-1
HARDCOVER ISBN: 978-1-5326-5707-8
EBOOK ISBN: 978-1-5326-5708-5

Cataloguing-in-Publication data:

Names: Peters, Greg, author

Title: Thomas à Kempis : his life and spiritual theology / Greg Peters.

Description: Eugene, OR: Cascade Books, 2021 | Series: Cascade Companions | Includes bibliographical references and index.

Identifiers: ISBN 978-1-5326-5706-1 (paperback) | ISBN 978-1-5326-5707-8 (hardcover) | ISBN 978-1-5326-5708-5 (ebook)

Subjects: LCSH: Kempis, Thomas à—1380–1471 | Spiritual life | Imitatio Christi | Monasticism and religious orders—History—Middle Ages, 600–1500.

Classification: C805.20.35 P48 2021 (paperback) | C805.20.35 (ebook)

02/17/21

*To my in-laws, Steven and Judith Burns,
devout believers and imitators of Jesus Christ*

CONTENTS

Introduction • ix

1 Thomas' Context: Late Medieval Monasticism and Spirituality • 1

2 The Brothers and Sisters of the Common Life and the Modern Devotion • 29

3 Thomas Hemerken à Kempis' Life and Formation • 51

4 Thomas' Spiritual Theology I: The Imitation of Christ • 67

5 Thomas' Spiritual Theology II: The Imitation of Christ • 101

6 The Ongoing Relevance of Thomas' Spirituality • 127

Conclusion • 139

APPENDIX
Translation of "The Life of Thomas à Kempis, Canon Regular" by Anonymous • 143

Bibliography • 149

Imitation of Christ *Index* • 161

Scripture Index • 163

Subject Index • 165

INTRODUCTION

THIS IS A BOOK about a book, more or less. In general it is an introduction (a "companion" according to the series title) to the thought of the late medieval monk and spiritual theologian Thomas à Kempis (d. 1471). Yet in many ways it is a study of his most important work, the *Imitation of Christ* (*Imitatio Christi*, in Latin), one of the bestselling books of all time,[1] which contains a treasure house of spiritual wisdom that can lead the reader to "true enlightenment and freedom from all blindness of heart."[2] Space will be given

---

1. Before 1500 there were over a hundred editions and between 1500 and 1650, there were 639 "identifiable" editions printed. See von Habsburg, *Catholic and Protestant Translations of the* Imitatio Christi, *1425–1650*, 1; and Staubach, "Thomas à Kempis," 690.

2. Thomas à Kempis, *Imitatio Christi* 1.1; in Sherley-Price, trans. *Thomas à Kempis*, 27. Subsequent references to the *Imitation of Christ* will be abbreviated parenthetically as follows: (1.5; 33); that is, the relevant book and chapter of the *Imitation* followed by the corresponding page number in Sherley-Price's translation. The original texts of Thomas' literary corpus are in Thomas Hemerken à Kempis, *Opera Omnia*.

Introduction

to Thomas' life and context and even though he wrote other works, I will dedicate this space to detailing the spiritual riches of the *Imitation of Christ*.

The *Imitation* has had a remarkable impact since its publication in the early fifteenth century (ca. 1420s), being translated into languages as diverse as Czech, Hungarian, Ukrainian, and Japanese, but also enjoying a popularity that cuts across Christian confessional lines. It "was appropriated by various Protestants from the south-west German and Swiss Protestant lands, and from Elizabethan and early Stuart England. The text's promotion by the [Roman Catholic] Society of Jesus was integral to its continued success," retaining "its pre-eminence in the seventeenth century."[3] It is hard to pinpoint the exact reason(s) for the *Imitation*'s popularity, but Johan Huizinga suggests it is because it "is not limited to one cultural epoch, . . . it departs from all culture and belongs to no culture in particular."[4] But Von Habsburg is right to note that "one should be wary of overemphasizing the so-called 'universality'" of the *Imitation* since this would divorce it from its "cultural boundaries."[5] More importantly, if the text is so "universal" then how is one to know how to read the text well?

Though he is primarily talking about the Sacred Scriptures, Thomas admonishes his readers that "we should as readily read simple and devout books as those that are lofty and profound. Do not be influenced by the importance of the writer, and whether his learning be great or small, but

---

3. Von Habsburg, *Catholic and Protestant Translations of the* Imitatio Christi, 1 and 179–242. The *Imitation* was first translated into English in the mid-fifteenth century. See Biggs, *The Imitation of Christ*.

4. Huizinga, *The Autumn of the Middle Ages*, 267.

5. Von Habsburg, *Catholic and Protestant Translations of the* Imitatio Christi, 2.

Introduction

let the love of pure truth draw you to read. Do not inquire, 'Who said this?' but pay attention to what is said" (1.5; 33). This, of course, is sage advice for readers of the Bible, but perhaps even more so for Thomas' *Imitation*. Yet, how does one read well, whether the books be simple and devout or lofty and profound? Given that the book in your hand is about a book, then it matters how the book's author tells us to read. As it turns out, Thomas' *Imitation* is one of those aforementioned simple and devout books. Thus, like the Holy Scriptures, the *Imitation* should be read with "humility, simplicity, and faith." Moreover, it should be read with "no concern to appear learned" (1.5; 33).

More will be said about these proper reading virtues, but from the outset it is important to note that the *Imitation of Christ* is meant to be read. That is, do not merely read this companion to the *Imitation* but read the *Imitation* itself in conjunction with this introduction. Even more importantly, do not just read this book and the *Imitation*, strive to *put them into practice* for "Lofty words do not make a man just or holy; but a good life makes him dear to God" (1.1; 27). In fact, according to Thomas, there is a reciprocal relationship between reading with understanding and doing. First, the way we live affects how we understand and delight in our reading: "Whoever desires to understand and take delight in the words of Christ must strive to conform his whole life to Him" (1.1; 27). Second, our reading, when done well, affects our lives. For example, "what holy precepts and godly exercises of divine teaching are proposed to us by Moses: to be worthily followed also by all the faithful."[6] In the end, however, it is not the reading itself that really matters; or, to say it differently, the word that ultimately matters is Jesus Christ *the* Word, for he "is the master of all: He the book

6. Thomas à Kempis, *Novice Sermons* 1.3; Scully, trans., *Sermons to the Novices Regular*, 21.

Introduction

and rule of religious: He the commentary of monks: He the text and glossary of decrees. He is the pattern of life for clerics, the instruction of laymen; the light of the faithful, the joy of the just, the glory of the angels: the end and consummation of all the desires of the saints."[7] Jesus Christ is *the* book of books, if you will, and, therefore, worthy of all imitation.

To show this Christ-centered emphasis in Thomas, this book will be a general introduction to his life and thought. He will be situated historically as a member of the Sisters and Brothers of the Common Life, the Modern Devotion, and the monastic Augustinian Canons of the Windesheim Congregation, which will itself be situated historically within the larger development of late medieval Christian monasticism and spirituality. A detailed exposition of his spiritual theology will be given, by making use of the *Imitation*. A concluding chapter will examine Thomas' contemporary relevance.

Though Thomas believed that it was Jesus himself who was the most important book for us to "read," he himself claimed (or at least it was claimed about him) that the only place he could find peace was in a corner with a book: "I have sought everywhere for peace, but I have found it not, save in nooks and in books."[8] It is true that Thomas lived a long and, at times, busy life, perhaps to some degree even one that ran contrary to his own idea of how to imitate Christ. Twenty-first-century readers of Thomas are even more challenged to find the kind of peace that a faithful *imitatio Christi* may yield. But may we find a nook nonetheless, one that will allow us the freedom to read about

---

7. Thomas à Kempis, *Novice Sermons* 1.3; Scully, trans., *Sermons to the Novices Regular*, 25–26.

8. Cited in Wright and Sinclair, *A History of Later Latin Literature*, 361.

Introduction

Thomas and to read his *Imitatio* so that we cannot only find peace but do the hard work of imitating Jesus Christ.

A final note: I am fortunate to have two reading nooks. My first reading nook is actually two places in my home, only one of which is an actual nook, the other being a home office. In both of these places I am not only surrounded by books but, more importantly, by the three most important people in my life: my wife Christina and my sons, Brendan and Nathanael. The best thing about reading at home is having these three nearby. Their love and support make my reading life possible. My office at Biola University, despite its book-, paper-, and memorabilia-laden appearance, is my other nook—my reading and writing haven. Its functionality far eclipses its form, but it is my home away from home. My colleagues at Biola University in the Torrey Honors College not only contribute to this amenable atmosphere but also model for me each and every day what it means to imitate Jesus. I am thankful for these godly friendships and for their ongoing support; to Matthew J. J. Hoskin, for his translation of the anonymous life of Thomas found in the Appendix; and to Robin Parry, my patient and encouraging editor at Wipf and Stock.

The majority of this book was written while on sabbatical from the Torrey Honors College of Biola University. I wish to thank Dr. Deborah Taylor, Provost; Dr. Melissa Schubert, Dean of Humanities and Social Sciences; and Dr. Paul Spears. Director of the Torrey Honors College, for their support in granting me a sabbatical. Much of the sabbatical was spent as a Visiting Scholar of the Von Hügel Institute, St. Edmund's College in the University of Cambridge. I am thankful to Dr. Philip McCosker, FRSA, Director of the Von Hügel Institute, and to its staff for their support during my stay; as well as the staff of the Divinity Faculty Library. As always, my wife Christina and sons, Brendan and

Introduction

Nathanael, provided the necessary distractions while working on the manuscript while also giving me the space necessary to pursue my vocation. Lastly, this book is dedicated to Steve and Judith Burns, my in-laws, for more than two and a half decades of support and encouragement and for their continuous and faithful devotion to and imitation of Jesus Christ. Like Christ, they too are worthy of imitation.

1

THOMAS' CONTEXT

Late Medieval Monasticism and Spirituality

THE HISTORY OF MONASTICISM is more complicated than it is often presented in general surveys of Christian history.[1] There is a historiography that wrongly and simplistically asserts that monasticism *started* in the fourth century with Anthony of Egypt (d. 356) founding what is called anchoretic monasticism while the former solider Pachomius (d. 348) is the founder of cenobitic monasticism.[2] More

1. For overviews of monastic history see Peters, *The Story of Monasticism;* and Rapley, *The Lord as Their Portion.*

2. Anchoretic monks (from the Greek *anchōreō*, meaning "to separate oneself, withdraw") are also known as "eremitical" monks, which is the most common designation of monks living solitary lives or in loose-knit communities. "Eremitical" comes from the Greek word *eremos,* meaning "desert," which is also the root of the English

accurately, monasticism began to *flourish* in the fourth century, though its origins remain obscure. There were monastic-like Jewish sects at the time of Jesus (e.g., the Essenes) and Greek and Roman philosophical schools of thought that engaged in activities that appear "monastic" (e.g., the Stoics and the Therapeutae). Moreover, non-Christian monasticism predates Christianity by centuries. For example, in Buddhism, as far back as the sixth or seventh century BCE, there were men known as *shramanas* (wanderers) who fasted to an extreme degree, remained naked to the elements, sat in freezing winter rivers, meditated in the summer heat surrounded by four fires, did not speak for years, and sat sleepless in contorted postures.[3] As Christianity made its way beyond the Roman Empire, Christian missionaries likely encountered these non-Christian monastics, possibly influencing Christian ascetic and monastic practices. And, of course, the earliest Christians engaged in a kind of lifestyle that would, in time, be labeled "monastic" (cf. Acts 2:44–46 and 4:32).

By the end of the fourth century, Christian monasticism was booming and maturing. There are reports in the church history of Palladius (d. ca. 425) and the writings of John Cassian (d. 435) that some cenobitic monasteries in the Egyptian desert had thousands of monks and there were also thousands of eremitical monks, so much so that Athanasius of Alexandria (d. 373) writes that the desert was made a city it was so populous.[4] These monks lived as

---

word "hermit." Monks who live in community are known historically as cenobites, with their form of life termed cenobitic. "Cenobitic" has its roots in the Greek words *koinos* ("common") and *bios* ("life"); therefore, cenobitism means "life in common."

3. See Thurman, "Tibetan Buddhist Perspectives on Asceticism."

4. Athanasius of Alexandria, *Life of Anthony* 15.

hermits, cenobites, lavrites (monks who lived in a *lavra*),[5] and even as stylites (those who lived atop columns), soon spreading into the areas of modern day Turkey, Syria, and Palestine, to name a few. At the same time, what started as a movement in the Middle East spread northward into Georgia, Armenia, and, in the late tenth century, Russia; eastward into the Arabian peninsula; southward to Ethiopia; and westward to Greece, Italy, and Gaul (modern France).

The Latin monasticism that gave birth to Augustinian canons like Thomas à Kempis derived primarily from those forms of monasticism that based themselves either on the rule of Benedict of Nursia (d. 547) or the so-called "rule" of Augustine of Hippo (d. 430). Benedict's rule, which was originally written for the monastery of Monte Cassino in southern Italy, became the main rule for cenobitic monasteries across Europe (especially for the Benedictines and the Cistercians). This prioritization and popularization of Benedict's rule began under the imperial leadership of Charlemagne (d. 814) and the monastic oversight of Benedict of Aniane (d. 821), reaching its climax and superiority around the twelfth century. Other communities, especially those of canons regular and many of the mendicant orders (e.g., the Franciscans and Dominicans), adopted the "rule" of Augustine, championed and propagated by Chrodegang of Metz (d. 766), in particular.[6] Benedict's rule is a combination of both spiritual teaching (e.g., the ladder of humility) and legislative guidelines (e.g., how to choose an abbot or

---

5. The Greek word *laura* means "lane" or "alley" and originally referred to the paths that connect individual monastic cells to a main, centralized church. In time, the term came to designate the whole monastic complex. In lavriotic monasteries, the monks spend the week praying, working, and eating in their individual cells, coming together only on Saturday and Sunday for a common liturgy.

6. Around 397 Augustine wrote a rule, but this is not the form of his extant rule. See below for a full discussion.

how many psalms to chant in the summer), whereas Augustine's rule is much shorter, concerning itself primarily with the love of God above all else.

Christian monasticism flourished wildly in the high and late Middle Ages, in both the eastern and western Christian churches. Tens of thousands of men and women joined monastic communities or lived solitary lives, dedicated to the single-minded pursuit of God. The monastic form of life became so commonplace that it could be critiqued by Dante Alighieri (d. 1321) and satirized and caricatured by the likes of Geoffrey Chaucer (d. 1400). With the advent of the Reformation and, in due time, the Enlightenment, the institution of monasticism fell on hard times, to say the least. Reformational Christians saw little value in monastic life, choosing instead to prioritize the baptism and priesthood of all believers to the effect that most monasteries were dissolved. The trend continued into later centuries, with monasteries suppressed, sometimes violently, under the regimes of Napoleon (d. 1821), the Bolsheviks, and Francisco Franco (d. 1975), for example. The theological changes brought about in the Roman Catholic Church at the Second Vatican Council (1962–65) precipitated, for various reasons, an exodus of men and women from the monastic life too. Nonetheless, monasticism remains an active presence in the church and the world today.

LATE MEDIEVAL MONASTICISM: INTRODUCTION

Beginning in the 1080s Western Christian monasticism underwent an exceptional season of expansion and growth.[7] In 1084 Bruno of Cologne (d. 1101) founded the Carthusians about thirty miles away from Grenoble, France and in

7. In general, see Lawrence, *Medieval Monasticism*.

1098 Robert of Molesme (d. 1111), who had trained Bruno of Cologne in the monastic life, left his Benedictine community to found a reformed community, later known as the Cistercians, at Cîteaux, also in eastern France.[8] In the subsequent decades, other men and women founded new monastic communities and/or monastic orders. Examples include the Gilbertines in England, founded by Gilbert of Sempringham (d. 1189) in 1131 and the abbey of Fontevraud in France, founded by Robert of Arbrissel (d. 1116) in 1100/1101.[9] Though originally founded in 1036 at Vallombrosa (just east of Florence, Italy) by John Gualbert (d. 1073), the Vallombrosan monasteries expanded rapidly in the first half of the twelfth century under the leadership of Abbot Bernard degli Uberti (d. 1133).[10] Similar to Vallombrosa, the monastery of Camaldoli was founded (by Romuald of Ravenna [d. 1027]) in the early eleventh century (between 1012–24) but grew rapidly between the late eleventh and early fourteenth centuries.[11] Notable later examples include the Benedictine Silvestrines founded by Silvestro Guzzolini (d. 1267) in 1231 and the Benedictine Olivetan reform near Siena, Italy in 1313 by Bernard Tolomei (d. 1348).[12]

THE ORDER OF THE HERMITS OF ST. AUGUSTINE

Though others could be cited, the more important foundations for the life and thought of Thomas à Kempis are

8. Wickstrom, "Carthusians," 244–47; and Lekai, *The Cistercians*.

9. Golding, *Gilbert of Sempringham and the Gilbertine Order*; and Bienvenu, "Aux origins d'un ordre religieux."

10. Meade, "From Turmoil to Solidarity."

11. Vigilucci, *Camaldoli*, 1–52.

12. Penco, *Storia del monachesimo in Italia*, 301–5 and 312–23.

the Augustinian hermits and the canons regular of Windesheim. The Order of the Hermits of St. Augustine (OESA) is the result of the actions of Pope Innocent IV, who, in 1243, began to combine existing groups of hermits that followed the *Rule of Augustine*,[13] a task completed by his successor Alexander IV with the "Great Union" of 1256. These hermits were changed into a mendicant (i.e., begging) order, charged with pastoral care and theological education. The origins of the Augustinian hermits is one of both fact and legend, born out of the debate between the Augustinian canons and the Augustinian hermits about who were the true and original "Order of St. Augustine": "The origins of the OESA's identity as the true sons of Augustine can be dated to the developments leading to and surrounding the order's privileges granted by Pope John XXII and his bull *Veneranda sanctorum* of 1327.... This resulted in a propaganda war between the Hermits and the Canons over which was the original Order of St. Augustine."[14] The debate initially began because the pope granted the OESA joint custody of Augustine of Hippo's tomb and, thereby, his body in Pavia. Textually, the debate was centered upon the *Sermons to the Brothers in the Desert* (*Sermones ad fratres in eremo*), from the early fourteenth century, a spurious and fabricated set of sermons "by Augustine" that made the case for the superiority of the OESA.[15]

In the fourth sermon of the collection, titled "On Prudence," the author bases himself on Augustine's authentic Sermon 355: "First Sermon on the Way of Life of his Clergy." In this sermon, preached around Christmas 425 or

13. See below for a discussion of the *Rule of Augustine*.

14. Saak, *Creating Augustine*, 58.

15. See Saak, *Creating Augustine*, 81–137. See also Saak, *High Way to Heaven*, 221: the "origin of these sermons remain in a fog of uncertainty."

Epiphany 426, though talking about events from the 390s, Augustine of Hippo describes how he and others came to North Africa with the intention of founding a monastery: "I ... came to this city [i.e., Hippo] as a young man.... I was looking for a place to establish a monastery, and live there with my brothers." Before he knew it, however, Augustine was "caught" and made a priest (in 391) and consecrated bishop in 395 by Valerius, Augustine's predecessor, who then provided land in the desert for Augustine on which to build his new monastery.[16] In the original sermon Augustine refers to the land grant as a *hortus* (garden), but the anonymous author of the *Sermons to the Brothers in the Desert* changes it to *heremo* (desert). In his hands Augustine's Sermon 355 reads,

> I came to the city of Hippo.... I came with confidence with my dearest friends.... [B]ringing nothing of wealth with me and with the grace of God as my help, I received the exceeding good will of that Valerius, and having set to work with much labour segregated from the people in a deserted place (*in heremo*), I began to build a monastery and with much anxiety I began to gather together into one servants of God living in the wilderness [*nemora*]. And thus I began equally to live with you according to the apostolic rule, having all things in common, and owning nothing as our own,... and I was forced to be made a priest bishop. And since I was not able to be with you here, I wanted to have my priests with me in the episcopal residence, and I began to live equally with them.[17]

---

16. Augustine of Hippo, *Sermon* 355, 2; Hill, trans., *Essential Sermons*, 407.

17. Saak, *Creating Augustine*, 120.

For the anonymous author of Sermon 4, the "issue of when and where Augustine founded his first monastery and for whom he wrote his Rule was the issue of contention between the Hermits and the Canons, with the Hermits trying to show that Augustine founded his order before he was ordained."[18] Since all Augustinian canons are priests, a group of lay men living first as hermits and only afterwards in the episcopal house in Hippo as priests means that they could not have been the precursors of the ordained Augustinian canons. But they could, under these circumstances, be the forerunners of the Augustinian hermits. The anonymous author of the *Sermons to the Brothers in the Desert* says similar things elsewhere to emphasize the point. Sermons 13 and 21 are particularly relevant.

In Sermon 13 the anonymous author has Augustine claim he was the founder of three monasteries after arriving in North Africa: "I was deemed worthy with praise to establish three monasteries in Hippo." The first is described as a hermitage in which "we have happily resided content with little indeed."[19] The second is the monastery *in horto* (in the garden) given to Augustine by Valerius. The third is at the episcopal residence. So, though Augustine lists one more monastery here than in Sermon 4, his iteration still supports that the hermits were founded first. In Sermon 21, "On the Three Types of Monks in Egypt," the anonymous author again returns to Augustine's founding of monasteries. For the first time we learn that Augustine's original African foundation was initially inhabited by monks from a monastery in Milan: "I went with complete love to Simplicianus . . . asking him on bended knee and with tears that he might give me some of his own servants of God, and these he gave me in a fatherly way. . . . Because he knew

18. Saak, *Creating Augustine*, 105.
19. Saak, *Creating Augustine*, 121.

that I wanted to build a monastery in Africa."[20] Augustine was given twelve men along with himself and three of his own friends. He continues, "thus I came to Africa . . . and I built a monastery, as you see, the very monastery in which we are now, in solitude, segregated from the crowd."[21] Though the number of original monks is new, the details of the first monastery are the same. All of this led Eric Saak to conclude that, in the end, any arguments in favor of the canons as being the first order founded by Augustine is simply "throwing bones" at them for "the Hermits were the only legitimate first-born sons of their father Augustine, the founder of the Order" and this could be proved by "Augustine's words themselves, words preached to his own hermits."[22] Nonetheless, the Augustinian canons did not just go away due to the growth and papal support of the hermits. In fact, they too experienced growth and renewal in the later Middle Ages.

THE WINDESHEIM CONGREGATION

Several years after the death of Geert Grote (d. 1384) the Brothers of the Common Life (see chapter 2) set to work quickly to fulfill one of Grote's wishes: founding a monastery. In the words of one of Grote's followers: "Three years after the death of Master Groote [sic], Master Florens [Radewijns] and his companions began to build the monastery in Windesheim (1387) and some of the disciples of Master Florens moved to Windesheim with his permission."[23] Near

20. Saak, *High Way to Heaven*, 122.
21. Saak, *High Way to Heaven*, 122.
22. Saak, *High Way to Heaven*, 226.
23. Cited in Post, *The Modern Devotion*, 293. Post's source is the *vita* of Grote written by Rudolph Dier, discussed in chapter 2. Post appears to have misread Dier's text because Dier says that it was

Zwolle, on land donated to them, five brothers began building a church and temporary living quarters, which were dedicated on October 17, 1387 and confirmed by the local bishop on December 13. The monks gave themselves over to manual labor (e.g., copying books for the library and choir), but lived mostly as solitaries, forgoing pastoral ministry. Over the first years the number of brothers in the monastery grew steadily, construction projects abounded, and benefactors generously supported the monastery. By 1392 the community was founding its first daughter house. R. R. Post writes, "Of much greater import, however, than the setting up of the above-mentioned monasteries, was the joining together of these three new foundations with Eemsteijn in 1394 or 1395 to form a close-knit monastic union. To use the current terminology, they form a congregation or chapter." That is, each community followed similar customs and usages and they "instituted a central authority which would make regulations, supervise all four monasteries, determine the actual situation by an annual visitation of each monastery separately and take appropriate measures."[24] From here growth was phenomenal, so much so that by the end of the fifteenth century there were nearly a hundred communities of men and women. Though the congregation died out in the early modern period, it "played a significant role in late medieval monastic reform, not least because it was not an outgrowth of an existing order but a new foundation emerging from the world of the laity."[25]

Ostensibly there was nothing of note vis-à-vis the founding of the monastery at Windesheim. Communities of Augustinian canons were common throughout Western Europe, especially from the eleventh century. The life of

"After two years . . . ."
 24. Post, *The Modern Devotion*, 296.
 25. Kollmann, "Windesheim Congregation," 500.

the canons regular was modelled on the *vita apostolica* and was, in essence, a hybrid order somewhere between priests dedicated to the active, clerical life and more contemplatively oriented monks. Hildebrand (d. 1085), the future Pope Gregory VII, had argued that the best life for priests was a life in common. Further, the monastic and church reformer Peter Damian (d. 1072) thought that all clergy serving in cathedral and university collegiate churches should renounce all private property and live a common life.[26] Both Hildebrand and Peter thought that this would allow the canons to live like the apostles by having all things in common, by living in community, and by praying together at fixed times. What was lacking in the early history of these canons regular was a rule. That would change in due time.

In the early ninth century, Chrodegang of Metz (d. 766) had written a *Rule for Canons* (*RC*) for the cathedral church in Metz, though he likely meant it as a model for others to follow. In the *RC*, Chrodegang relies heavily on the *Rule of Benedict*, hence from the start the canons had a monastic bent. Structurally,

> The Prologue introduces us to the rule, and, rehearsing a version of Christian history, it offers Chrodegang's interpretation of the obligations attendant on his office as bishop and lays out the reasons why he felt obliged to impose this new set of regulations on the life of the canons. The three middle sections of the rule are quite similarly structured, in that the first chapter of each (cc. 1, 12, and 20) sets forth the theme of the section, the central chapter (cc. 8, 14, and 25) is the most important and in a way exemplifies that theme, and the last chapters (cc. 11, 19, and 30) summarize the contents and goals of the section. The final section, in exploring the implications

26. Lawrence, *Medieval Monasticism*, 164.

of the previous thirty chapters, restates and extends the purpose and goals of the rule which were initially set out in the Prologue.[27]

In short, for Chrodegang the canonical life is one of 1) humility, manifested in faithful chapter attendance and good zeal; 2) penance and regular confession; and 3) balanced, appropriate asceticism under the oversight of approved leadership.

More importantly, for the later history of the canons regular, including the Congregation of Windesheim, was the so-called *Rule of Augustine*.[28] As we have it today, the *Rule of Augustine* is a document comprised of nine early documents, eight legislative texts, and one letter. Yet, in the end, there are really only three texts that make up the *Rule of Augustine*: the "Regulations for a Monastery," the "Rule" (*Praeceptum*) or the "Rule for Nuns" (*Regularis informatio*), and the "Reprimand to Quarrelling Nuns." Augustine's main inspiration for the monastic life comes from the practice of the earliest Christians: "Now the full number of those who believed were of one heart and soul, and no one said that any of the things that belonged to him was his own, but they had everything in common" (Acts 4:32). Using this basic biblical teaching as his foundation, Augustine continues by primarily expanding on this first principle. The community prays seven times a day and engages silently in meaningful work, but should also be given "leisure for reading."[29] No one is to own private property but instead to have all things in common, and the superior is obeyed with fidelity. The monks practice asceticism in moderation and

---

27. Claussen, *The Reform of the Frankish Church*, 60.

28. The history of the *Rule of Augustine* is quite unique and is detailed in Lawless, *Augustine of Hippo*.

29. Augustine of Hippo, "Regulations for a Monastery" 3; Lawless, *Augustine of Hippo*, 75.

to the "extent that . . . health allows."[30] Thus, the *Rule of Augustine* is a collection of precepts that justify the monastic life—love of God and neighbor—and explain how to live in community and how to be moderate in ascetical activity. It is this rule that, in the end, became the guiding principle of all the regular canons, including those at Windesheim.

Structurally the congregation was run by the Windesheim chapter, constituted from all the priors of the monasteries in the congregation. The chapter met annually in Windesheim at which they appointed twelve *definitores* (one who makes a ruling) "on the understanding that the prior of Windesheim, who was the prior superior of the entire chapter, was always in the deliberations."[31] The chapter appointed the *visitores* (those who visited the communities to ensure proper order and observance) and examined reports of past visitations. They appointed new priors from vacated seats and decided which communities, of the ones applying for affiliation, could join the congregation. All in all, the annual chapter dutifully conducted all the business that kept the congregation faithful in moving forward. Such a monastic system of government went back at least to the Cistercians in the twelfth century, but it was put to good effect at Windesheim, creating not only a uniformity of observance but by also curating an identifiable Windesheimian spirituality.

THE CLIMATE OF LATE MEDIEVAL SPIRITUALITY

The phrase "medieval spirituality" is deceptively simplistic. On the one hand even defining "spirituality" has a rich

---

30. Augustine of Hippo, "Rule" 3.1 and 4.1; Lawless, *Augustine of Hippo*, 35.

31. Post, *The Modern Devotion*, 308.

history, especially in the twentieth century.[32] Though it is easier to define the chronological limits of the Middle Ages, the adjective "medieval" includes a vast array of places, people, texts, and perspectives. Thus, by necessity, simply laying the groundwork for any kind of discussion of "late medieval spirituality" will be, to some extent, cursory. Nonetheless, such an endeavor is necessary in order to situate the thought of Thomas à Kempis. Again, at the risk of being overly reductionistic, I will chose to look at four streams of influence (though there are certainly more) that fed into the river of Thomas' thought and practice: 1) late medieval English spirituality; 2) Carthusian spirituality; 3) Beguine spirituality; and 4) Augustinian spirituality.[33]

For centuries there was a close connection between what we now know as England and the so-called "Low Countries." This connection was often one of commerce, wherein both regions entered into profitable business ventures, perhaps none more so than the sheep trade, primarily between the farmers of Yorkshire (esp. the Cistercian monasteries) and Flanders, the cloth-making capital of the high and late Middle Ages.[34] In time, especially in the fourteenth and fifteenth centuries, there were many cultural contacts as well, in the areas of music, books, and art.[35] To these

32. See, for example, Philip Sheldrake, "What Is Spirituality?"

33. My point here is not to suggest that Thomas made direct use of these sources. In fact, the "*Imitation* is . . . a highly derivative work[;] . . . the author used only works written before 1200, above all (in addition to the Bible and a few of the church fathers, primarily Augustine) those by Anselm, Bernard, Hugh and Richard of St Victor, William of St Thierry, and other twelfth-century writers" (Constable, *Three Studies in Medieval Religious and Social Thought*, 240). I am, rather, attempting to sketch an image of the environment in which Thomas lived and wrote.

34. Burton, *The Monastic Order in Yorkshire 1069–1215*.

35. See the essays in Barron and Saul, eds., *England and the Low Countries in the Late Middle Ages*.

types of contact one should also add religious—institutionally and textually. Thus, late medieval English spirituality impacted its eastern, continental neighbors and vice versa.[36]

Gordon Mursell, in his study of English spirituality, titles the time between 1300 and 1500 "The Quest for the Suffering Jesus," a quite accurate description for late medieval English spirituality.[37] By this time there was an active and enthusiastic recovery, even among the laity, of the sufferings of Jesus Christ at Calvary and an intentional attempt to imitate him. In England, the laity primarily worked out their spiritual lives in the context of the local parish by way of corporate prayer and liturgy, supplemented with private prayer and membership in particular guilds and confraternities. The most important spiritual writers from the era—including Richard Rolle (d. 1349), Walter Hilton (d. 1396), Julian of Norwich (d. 1416), and the anonymous authors of the *Cloud of Unknowing* (later fourteenth century) and the pseudo-Bonaventuran *Meditations on the Life of Christ* (early fourteenth century)[38]—each in their own way emphasize the *suffering* Christ, but each also advocate for an *interiorization* of spirituality. That is, a spirituality that is not institutionalized as much as experienced in one's inner being: "When you are in bed, go back to the beginning of the day, and look diligently *in your heart*: if you have done any evil, and there be sorry; if any good, and there give thanks to God."[39]

---

36. Davidson, "Northern Spirituality and the Late Medieval Drama of York," 129.

37. Mursell, *English Spirituality*, vi.

38. Translated into English by the Carthusian Nicholas Love (d. ca. 1424) as *The Mirror of the Blessed Life of Jesus Christ*.

39. Pantin, "Instructions for a Devout and Literate Layman," 400; italics added for emphasis.

The late medieval English emphasis on the suffering of Christ is evidenced in both art and text. For many centuries depictions of Jesus on the cross were rather domestic. Christ, at best, looked mildly uncomfortable; he certainly did not look like he was in pain. One of the earliest extant images of the crucifixion (ca. 430s), an image carved into wood doors at Santa Sabina in Rome, depicts the crucifixion, but without any visible crosses. Jesus and the two thieves appear in the *orans* position making it easy to miss that this is the crucifixion of Jesus. In England, "early Anglo-Saxon Crucifixions had represented Christ in a more or less formalized manner against the cross."[40] By the early fourteenth century, this had changed. For example, in 1338 a stained glass window was installed in York Minster that depicted Jesus on the cross, stretched out at a painful angle. Jesus' face evidences clear distress. In another window at the minster there is the "Mercy Seat Trinity" in which Jesus is depicted even more graphically, with blood spurting out of his side. These windows, of course, were meant to be looked at by those worshipping in the minster, thereby catechizing them as to the suffering of Christ on the cross. Many local, smaller churches also had similar images in their windows.

Textually, albeit in a way that bridges the distance between the text and its public hearing, a great example also comes from York, but this time in its passion play. As the four soldiers tasked with attaching Christ to the cross do their work, they notice the difficulty of stretching Jesus' limbs to the appropriate places on the cross in which holes for the nails have been pre-drilled. Their solution is to fasten a cord to Jesus' wrists and ankles and stretch him until he "fits." They banter,

---

40. Davidson, "Northern Spirituality and the Late Medieval Drama of York," 135.

> 1 SOLDIER: Ah, peace man, for Mahound,
> Let no man wot that strange thing,
> A rope shall tug him down
> Even if all his sinews go asunder.
>
> 2 SOLDIER: That cord full fittingly can I fasten,
> The comfort of this wretch to keel.
>
> 1 SOLDIER: Bind on then fast, that all be ready,
> It is no matter how terrible he feel.
>
> 2 SOLDIER: Lug on yet both a little yet.
>
> 3 SOLDIER: I shall not cease, as I have joy.
>
> 4 SOLDIER: And I shall attempt him for to hit.
>
> 2 SOLDIER: Oh, haul!
>
> 4 SOLDIER: Whoa, now, I hold it well.
>
> 1 SOLDIER: Stop, drive in that nail,
> So that no fault be found.
>
> 4 SOLDIER: This working would not fail
> If four bulls here were bound.
>
> 1 SOLDIER: These cords have severely increased his pains,
> Ere he were to the borings brought.[41]

Though the play continues in this vein, this modest example aptly demonstrates the vivid depiction of the pain and agony associated with Jesus offering himself for crucifixion. Nicholas Love's vernacular translation of the Italian *Meditations on the Life of Christ* is just as graphic:

> And so is that most innocent, fairest and cleanest flesh, flour[42] of all mankind altogether torn

---

41. Beadle and King, eds., *York Mystery Plays*, 216; modernized. The acting out the crucifixion was entrusted to the Pinners guild, those who made pins and nails. Their connection with crucifixion is clear.

42. White/pure as flour.

and full of wounds, running out on all sides that precious king's blood and so long beaten and scourged with wound upon wound and bruise upon bruise til both the lookers and the smiters were weary; and then was he given to be unbound.[43]

In the late medieval spiritual tradition of England, one of the best vernacular examples of this emphasis on the suffering Jesus is Richard Rolle's *Meditations on the Passion*. In one place he writes, "O lord, I can see your red blood coursing down your cheeks, torrents after each blow, down front and back. Your crown has torn to pieces the skin on your head, every thorn in it penetrates your skull."[44] For Rolle, meditation becomes a desire for imitation: "So, lord, if I can't be present there as one who has merited it, I request some share in your death as one of those who are guilty. . . . Come then, heavenly healer . . . and enlighten me as you know my need; kindle in my heart a tiny spark of your passion, of love and of compassion."[45] More so, Rolle inserts himself into the actual events of Calvary when he takes on the identify of a thief, like the two crucified with Christ: "Lord, in your mercy, you who are the fount of mercy, tell me who am your thief what you said to him, for I have stolen your good deeds, and abused your graces."[46] Again, meditation leads to a request for imitation, thus laying the foundation for an *imitatio Christi* along the lines found in Thomas à Kempis.[47] Though this kind of meditation on

43. Powell, ed., *The Mirror*, 229–30; modernized.

44. Allen, *Richard Rolle*, 94.

45. Allen, *Richard Rolle*, 104.

46. Allen, *Richard Rolle*, 101.

47. Hodapp, "Richard Rolle's Passion Meditations," 99: "The themes of Christ's humanity and poverty are developed by Rolle in order to lead readers to an imaginative *imitatio* exercise near the end of the meditations."

the suffering Jesus is found elsewhere (e.g., in the aforementioned translation of the *Meditations on the Life of Christ*), the English tradition, in particular, is rife with such literature and a spirituality of suffering.

In essence, there is only one kind of spirituality. As Hans Urs von Balthasar has argued, "all possible forms of Christian spirituality meet and so, through the medium of faith, flow into each other."[48] There may be various applications of the Christian way of life, but because there is only one gospel then there can be only one spirituality. However, adding an adjective can, at times, bring clarity or at least delimit the range of what one means. That is the case with "Carthusian spirituality." Though a medieval Carthusian would have simply thought of his spirituality as biblical, he would have surely known that there were certain unique elements to life in the Spirit for a Carthusian monk. In the words of James Hogg, "If there is no school of medieval Carthusian writers quite to match the early Cistercians, the Carthusians nevertheless made a significant—and often idiosyncratic—contribution to medieval spiritual literature."[49] Two Carthusians in particular influenced medieval spirituality and, in time, impacted Thomas à Kempis.

The first, Guigo II (d. 1188), wrote the *Ladder of Monks* in which he lays out the four rungs of the ladder that enable one to reach contemplation: 1) reading; 2) meditation; 3) prayer; and 4) contemplation. Guigo writes, "Reading seeks for the sweetness of a blessed life, meditation perceives it, prayer asks for it, contemplation tastes it."[50] Reading "is the careful study of the Scriptures. . . . Meditation is the busy application of the mind to seek the help of one's own reason

48. Von Balthasar, "The Gospel as Norm," 17.

49. Hogg, "Carthusian Spirituality," 27.

50. Guigo II, *Ladder of Monks* 3; Colledge and Walsh, trans., *The Ladder of Monks*, 82.

for knowledge of hidden truth. Prayer is the heart's devoted turning to God. . . . Contemplation is when the mind is in some sort lifted up to God and held above itself, so that it tastes the joys of everlasting sweetness."[51] Guigo's emphasis on reading, in particular, finds great resonance in Thomas.

Another Carthusian, Guigo de Ponte (d. 1297), is the author of *On Contemplation*, which "is not a methodically organized treatise, but resembles three extended conferences, which deal with the same material, giving different emphases in depicting the soul aspiring to union with God. All three books display the progress of the sinner to the ultimate degree of contemplation, the vision of God."[52] Guigo is clear that anyone who experiences contemplation, "especially at the level of tasting wisdom," has done so thanks to God alone who "granted this experience."[53] Nonetheless, each person must prepare himself for this gift of God. Guigo de Ponte adopts Guigo II's schema of reading, meditation, prayer, and contemplation, writing that one will move through these "levels" only if he purifies his sinful soul. In the end, one must recognize one's sinfulness and rebellion against God and thereafter make use of the four rungs of the ladder to prepare oneself for receiving God's gift of contemplation. Guigo's emphasis on sin is echoed by Thomas so much so that it seems clear that there is a stream of influence from the Carthusians to the fountain from which Thomas drank. Hogg, in one place, concludes that Guigo de Ponte, for example, did influence the Modern Devotion (see chapter 2 below), but only "indirectly" since "it cannot be denied that St. Bernard, St. Aelred of Rievaulx, and St. Anselm of Canterbury had preceded the Carthusian

51. Guigo II, *Ladder of Monks* 3; Colledge and Walsh, trans., *The Ladder of Monks*, 82.

52. Hogg, "Carthusian Spirituality," 43.

53. Guigo de Ponte, *On consideration* Prol; Martin, trans., *Carthusian Spirituality*, 173.

[i.e., Guigo] in this field."[54] But elsewhere Hogg writes, "the autobiographical tendency of a number of authors connected with the *Devotio Moderna* finds its parallel in the Carthusian tradition dating back to Guigo I's *Meditationes*."[55] Otto Gründler further notes Guigo's influence on Grote (founder of the Brothers and Sisters of the Common Life and subsequently the Modern Devotion and, by extension, the Windesheim Congregation), concluding that the list of books that influenced Grote "certainly shows the influence of the Carthusians."[56] Grote influenced Thomas, thereby so did the Carthusians, even if indirectly. In any case, there is a clear influence, especially when we consider that Grote spent three years of his life attached to the Carthusian monastery at Monnikhuizen near Arnhem. Grote himself said that the Carthusians were the most commendable of all the monastic orders and Thomas believed that despite the pervasiveness of worldly evil, the Carthusians retained the "heavenly light."[57]

Yet Thomas was not only influenced by late medieval English spiritual writers, religious art and practices, and the Carthusians, but also by groups of lay women and men known respectively as the Beguines and Beghards that started in the thirteenth century, primarily in urban centers. Just as traditional religious orders were being founded in an attempt to emulate the "apostolic life" (*vita apostolica*; e.g., Franciscans and Dominicans), lay women and men sought to do the same, but outside the confines of any

---

54. Hogg, "Carthusian Spirituality," 45.

55. Hogg, "The English Charterhouses and the Devotio Moderna," 261; italics in the original.

56. Gründler, "*Devotio moderna atque antiqua*," 32 and 35.

57. Hogg, "The English Charterhouses and the Devotio Moderna," 259.

recognized religious order.[58] Some Beguines and Beghards lived apostolically at home with their family whereas others lived together in semi-monastic communities, but they did now follow a formal rule. In short, these men and women sought what traditional monks and friars had but without formal recognition. Women in particular were drawn to this type of life, agreeing not to marry while they lived as Beguines, imitating the life of Jesus through their poverty and devotion.[59] In the words of John Van Engen, "urban women entered upon lives of spiritual intensity in phenomenal numbers, most unprofessed, living as recluses and in quietude, though also active in hospices and almshouses. . . . [T]hese unprofessed converts came to be called 'beguines.'"[60]

The beguine movement began in 1215 when the theologian Jacques de Vitry (d. 1240) secured from Pope Honorius III a papal dispensation for women who were living together in chastity and poverty. Jacques was greatly influenced by Marie d'Oignies (whose life he wrote in 1215, two years after her death), who lived in Liège. Marie was married at fourteen but convinced her husband that they should divest themselves of their goods, live together celibately, and care for lepers. Several years later, with her husband's permission, she left him and settled with a community of women not far from a house of Augustinian canons where she remained until her untimely death at the age of thirty-six. Jacque's original purpose in writing Marie's life was to fight the Albigensian heresy. It "was written to be a shining example of the fact that it was possible to be holy, devout and pure even within the Catholic Church."[61]

58. Grundmann, *Religious Movements in the Middle Ages*.
59. See Simons, *Cities of Ladies*.
60. Van Engen, *Sisters and Brothers of the Common Life*, 21.
61. Murk-Jansen, *Brides in the Desert*, 25.

Thomas' Context

Though Marie was not the first Beguine, having joined an already established community (i.e., a Beguinage), she became the paradigm for the Beguine lifestyle. The Beguines were particularly prevalent in northern Europe, especially in the Low Countries, which, as we will see in chapter 2, was the homeland of the Modern Devotion that gave birth to Thomas à Kempis.[62]

The Beguines almost always wrote in the vernacular, thereby making their books easily available to the "average" lay person. "To modern eyes," writes Saskia Murk-Jansen, "much of the Beguine's work appears to be intensely personal, but it is important to remember that it is above all didactic literature. The women were writing to teach others and the texts were intended as spiritual guidance for their communities."[63] One common theme in Beguine spiritual writing is suffering as a form of *imitatio Christi*. The Beguine Mechthild of Magdeburg (d. 1282) writes that she is God's joy but "he is my torment."[64] Further, suffering is a spiritual drink that brings health to the one who consumes it:

> I am ill and I long deeply
> For the health-giving draught
> Which Jesus Christ Himself drank...[65]
> This health-giving draught pleases me
> The draught of suffering-for-the-love-of-God.

---

62. There were hundreds of Beguinages in the Low Countries and Germany. See Van Engen, *Sisters and Brothers of the Common Life*, 22.

63. Van Engen, *Sisters and Brothers of the Common Life*, 35–36.

64. Menzies, *The Revelations of Mechthild of Magdeburg*, 10.

65. This is certainly an echo of Jesus' words during his suffering in the Garden of Gethsemane, for example: "And going a little farther he fell on his face and prayed, saying, 'My Father, if it be possible, let this cup pass from me; nevertheless, not as I will, but as you will'" (Matt 26:39).

> Suffering is bitter so we add a herb to it—
> Glad-suffering: and a second called Patience-in-suffering
> These too are bitter and so we add another herb
> Holy Fervour: that makes Patience sweet
> As well as everything we do;
> It helps us to wait long in suffering . . .
>
>> Ah dear Lord! wouldst Thou but give me this draught
>> I should live unwearied with Joy in suffering . . . .[66]

Hadewijch (d. 1248), a Flemish Beguine, also frequently notes the role of suffering in spiritual growth. In one of her poems she writes,

> In all things may God be your consolation,
> And make known to you the taste of Love—
> By which you can suffer everything— . . .
> Love—himself—is best honored
> By sufferings from which many a person gladly flees . . .
> If you wish to approach sublime Love
> And learn her ways perfectly,
> You must always, with burning eagerness,
> Seek new sufferings for Love's sake.
> You must let Love—himself—act;
> He will repay all pain with love.
> If you let your sufferings be a burden to you,
> You do not love him, that is evident. . . .
> Come, desire to suffer in order to ascend,
> So that we together in one knowledge
> May have fruition of our Love.[67]

For Hadewijch, the only way to fully imitate Christ and to be one with him is to share "unequivocally the humanity of

---

66. Menzies, *The Revelations of Mechthild of Magdeburg*, 232–33.
67. Hart, trans., *Hadewijch*, 328–29.

Thomas' Context

Christ."[68] Thus, just as he suffered, all who desire to imitate him must suffer too. This theme anticipates Thomas' *Imitation*, who lived in close proximity to many Beguines and was influenced by them.[69]

The last area of influence is Augustinian spirituality. This is the most direct influence of medieval spirituality on Thomas since he was a member of the Augustinian House of Canons at Windesheim.[70] Here it is prudent to sketch in general outline the contours of Augustinian spirituality. But first it should be noted that the adjective "Augustinian" has a troubled history and lacks precision. In general, "Augustinian" literally refers to anything having to do with the history or thought of Augustine of Hippo, whether that history or thinking is genuine or not.[71] As shown above, Augustine's monastic lifestyle was "eremetized" (i.e., turned into a form of living in the desert, whether real or imagined) in order to justify the existence and raison d'être of the medieval OESA. There are also the pseudo-Augustinian texts that circulated throughout the Middle Ages that purport to present the thought of the fifth-century bishop of Hippo. Nonetheless, despite the fraught history of "Augustinian" or "Augustinianism" there is still a discernible "Augustinian spirituality." And though there are different areas that could be explored, I will limit myself to the concept of *interiority*, for Augustine "is the founder of a specifically Western tradition of interiority or inwardness, embracing three interrelated concepts: inner

68. Murk-Jansen, *Brides in the Desert*, 98.

69. Goudriaan, *Piety in Practice and Print*, 112–34.

70. See Van Geest. "Order, Desire and Grace."

71. On this dichotomy between the genuine Augustine and the "created" Augustine see the cleverly titled *Creating Augustine* by E. L. Saak.

self, inward turn, and outward signs as expressions of inner things."[72]

In his well-known and profoundly influential work, the *Confessions*, Augustine acknowledges that he does not know himself because he is behind himself. The image is a powerful one, for how can someone see themselves if they are behind themselves. Even if you turn around you are always putting your back to yourself. Augustine needed to find a way to move himself from behind himself to be in front of himself. As it turns out, that meant not a turning around toward himself but a going *into* himself. Interestingly, Augustine says that he learned this from the Neo-Platonists: "By the Platonic books I was admonished to return into myself. With you [God] as my guide I entered into my innermost citadel."[73] Yet this inner movement is made possible ultimately by God, even if its inspiration comes by way of pagan Greek philosophers. Augustine writes, "let me confess what I know of myself. Let me confess too what I do not know of myself. For what I know of myself I know because you grant me light, and what I do not know of myself, I do not know until such time as my darkness becomes 'like noonday' before your face."[74] For Augustine, we must move *intra se* (into ourselves) before we can move *extra se* (outside ourselves). The way to God (and the way out of himself) was, for Augustine, an interior movement, for God is within each person.[75] The Christian believer descends into herself in order to ascend to God.[76] Just after

---

72. Cary, "Interiority," 454.

73. Augustine of Hippo, *Confessions* 7.10.16; Chadwick, trans., *Saint Augustine: Confessions*, 123.

74. Augustine of Hippo, *Confessions* 10.5.7; Chadwick, trans., *Saint Augustine: Confessions*, 183.

75. See Augustine of Hippo, *Confessions* 10.27.38.

76. Laird, "Augustinian Spirituality," 59: "For Augustine, the interior journey finds its consummation not in ourselves but in God."

his profound conversion Augustine summarizes succinctly this interiority when he writes,

> You took me up from behind my own back where I had placed myself because I did not wish to observe myself (Ps. 20:13), and you set me before my face (Ps. 49:21) so that I should see how vile I was, how twisted and filthy, covered in sores and ulcers. . . . If I and you once again placed me in front of myself; you thrust me before my own eyes so that I should discover my iniquity and hate it.[77]

Again, through sin Augustine put himself behind himself but by grace God turns him around and sets aright what had been made wrong.

This Augustinian emphasis on interiority becomes a hallmark of medieval spirituality, especially, for example, among the twelfth-century Cistercians, such as Bernard of Clairvaux and William of St-Thierry.[78] Moreover, in the late Middle Ages there were many Augustinian canons active in promoting the interior spirituality of Augustine. For example, Michael of Massa (d. 1327), an Italian Augustinian hermit, produced a life of Christ that has been shown to be the most influential work on the Carthusian Ludolph of Saxony's (d. 1378) *Life of Christ*, which heavily influenced the *Devotio Moderna* and, by extension, Thomas à Kempis.[79] Thus, an Augustinian spirituality of interiority made its way from the bishop of Hippo in the fifth century to Thomas in the fifteenth century. This emphasis on interiority manifests itself repeatedly throughout the *Imitation of Christ*.

77. Augustine of Hippo, *Confessions* 8.7.16; Chadwick, trans., *Saint Augustine: Confessions*, 144.

78. See Kramer, *Sin, Interiority, and Selfhood in the Twelfth-Century West*.

79. Zumkeller, "The Spirituality of the Augustinians," 67.

DISCUSSION QUESTIONS

1. Early manifestations of monasticism interpreted Augustine's words to mean different things to support their cause. What do you take Augustine's view of monasticism to be?

2. How does one achieve contemplation and what is the purpose of contemplation?

3. What is the importance of interiorization and introspection?

4. How can you adopt a spirit of Christian suffering and/or a spirit of Christian interiority?

2

THE BROTHERS AND SISTERS OF THE COMMON LIFE AND THE MODERN DEVOTION

INTRODUCTION

IN 1881 GERMAN HISTORIAN Karl Grube wrote a book on the late medieval Augustinian canon and chronicler of the Windesheim Congregation Johannes Busch (d. ca. 1480).[1] There, in a section titled "Sources and Proofs," Grube writes, "Clemens Leeder, geb. 1782, ord. 1806, Domlector zu Hildesheim 1834, † am 4. November 1865."[2] In other words, Clemens Leeder was born in 1782 and ordained a priest in 1806. He became Domlector (theologian) at Hildesheim Cathedral in 1834 and died in 1865. From this

---

1. Grube, *Johannes Busch, Augustinerpropst zu Hildesheim*.
2. Grube, *Johannes Busch*, 282.

it does not necessarily seem that Leeder was a terribly important person. He was likely a dutiful priest and member of the cathedral community, but no books have been written about him nor does it appear that he wrote any books. Yet, Leeder is the last in a long line of men, going all the way back to 1386; for he has the distinction of being the last canon of the congregation of Windesheim before its demise.[3] In other words, Leeder (nineteenth century) was a direct spiritual brother, if you will, of Thomas à Kempis (fourteenth/fifteenth century).

The road between Thomas and Leeder was a long and winding one for sure. The monastery at Windesheim itself was dissolved in 1581 though the congregation continued for nearly three more centuries. At its height in the late fourteenth/early fifteenth century there were nearly a hundred communities in the congregation, both of men and women. The Reformation, of course, took its toll on the congregation, especially since so many of the communities were subsequently located in Protestant areas. The congregation was reorganized by Pope Gregory XIII in 1573 but by 1728 there were only thirty-two communities left. In 1790, Emperor Joseph II closed eleven houses in what was then the Austrian Netherlands and Napoleon closed more in the early nineteenth century.[4] Thus, by Leeder's death in 1865 there were no more monasteries in the Windesheim Congregation, a shadow of its former glory.

---

3. It should be noted, however, that the congregation was revived in 1961.

4. See van der Woude, ed., *Acta capituli Windeshemensis*; and Hendrikman et al., eds. *Windesheim 1395–1995*.

BROTHERS AND SISTERS OF THE COMMON LIFE

The story of the Brothers and Sisters of the Common Life begins with the preaching of Master Geert Grote in the 1370s. Born in 1340, Grote spent the first part of his life chasing after prestigious and lucrative church appointments. Orphaned as a ten year old, Grote went to the University of Paris where he earned a master's degree in 1358. He repeatedly applied, to some avail, to the papal curia, then in residence in Avignon, France, for church income. It appears that in the mid-1360s he was studying law and possibly theology, also in Paris, and by the late 1360s and early 1370s he had obtained prebends (i.e., revenues) by being a canon at both Aachen and Utrecht. Yet, around 1374 Grote had a change of heart. Finding his life "unclean" he decided to make a "turn." So, in September 1374 he made his family home in Deventer available to a community of religious women, à la the Beguines, and by October 1375 he had given up his benefices.[5] In his own words, Grote promised

> to order my life to the glory, honor, and service of God and to the salvation of my soul; to put no temporal good of body, position, fortune, or learning ahead of my soul's salvation; and to pursue the imitation of God in every way consonant with learning and discernment and with my own body and estate, which predispose certain forms of imitation.[6]

Drawing up a document he called "Resolutions and Intentions, but Not Vows," Grote determined to 1) "desire no further office or income"; 2) "practice none of the forbidden sciences"; 3) to give up the "lucrative disciplines" of

---

5. Van Engen, *Sisters and Brothers of the Common Life*, 12.
6. Van Engen, *Devotio moderna*, 65.

medicine, civil law, or canon law; 4) "return to learning" (i.e., theological learning) but not to earn a degree; 5) attend Mass every day, if possible; 6) practice abstinence from food and drink; and 7) live unhurriedly, thoughtfully, and simply.[7] Following his "turn," Grote spent time from 1374-77 with the Carthusians near Arnheim, but decided not to join them. Instead, he was ordained a deacon and went on "self-made preaching tours (late 1379-fall 1383), making converts."[8] His fiery sermons against the ills of the church, especially simony (the buying and selling of church offices and the power that came with these positions), earned him an episcopal prohibition against preaching in 1383. Forbidden to preach, Grote gathered a group of adherents together at his house in Deventer for spiritual discussions. He died from the plague on August 20, 1384.

Though Grote himself never formally entered a monastery (his stay with the Carthusians for three years was as a guest), he was favorable to the monastic life: Grote

> tends to regard and use the monastery as a sort of charitable institution. He does, however, make the obedience and devotion of the candidate conditions for recommendation, and leaves the final decision to the head of the monastery. He certainly respects the monasteries and the life of the monks, to whom he recommends his friends. . . . Yet he does not automatically regard the monastic life for everyone as superior to the task in the world.[9]

From this we see that Grote was not so enamored of the monastic life that he espoused it for everyone. In fact, a

---

7. Van Engen, *Devotio moderna*, 65-75.

8. Van Engen, *Sisters and Brothers of the Common Life*, 13.

9. Post, *The Modern Devotion*, 60. Cf. Van Zijl, *Gerard Grote*, 206-32.

number of his extant letters are written to recipients whom he is trying to dissuade from entering the monastic life. For example, in a letter to his friend John Oude Scutte he writes, "I dare not advise you to enter a monastery. Not that I lack confidence in this way of the Lord, but I desire that you should remain in the world, without being of the world. There are religious[10] who are of the world."[11] Nonetheless, though Grote does not advocate that everyone should enter a monastery per se, he does not think terribly highly of marriage.

Just before his untimely death, he wrote the treatise *On Matrimony*.[12] The work is addressed to a canon of Cologne who, at an advanced age, desired to marry. Grote dissuades him from leaving his life of study at such an advanced age. Moreover, the canon is living a more perfect life and he should not, therefore, marry, thereby adopting a less perfect manner of life. Marriage exists, says Grote, for two reasons: the procreation of children and to prevent fornication. But he also thinks that even procreation should be limited since it is possible to bring bad children into the world, the desire to marry only to procreate is animalistic and Grote is not convinced that marriage prevents fornication. A married man can still lust after a woman who is not his wife, and vice versa. As R. R. Post rightfully notes, Grote does not seem to consider that marriage can be an expression of love and that marriage strengthens the bonds of love between a

---

10. The term "religious" is, at times, used synonymously with "monk." However, in later usage a "monk" is someone who lives cloistered in a monastery whereas a "religious" is someone living under vows but who does not live in a monastery. For example, there are Benedictine and Carthusian monks, whereas Franciscan and Dominican friars, for example, are not monks but members of non-monastic religious orders, hence they are "religious."

11. Post, *The Modern Devotion*, 64.

12. See Van Zijl, *Gerard Grote*, 195–205.

man and woman. M. A. Mulders, editor of *On Matrimony*, concludes that the views found in the treatise, despite what Grote says elsewhere, represents his general thoughts about marriage—that it is to be avoided when possible.[13]

This likely explains why Grote gathered some followers together in his home in 1383, expecting to found a religious community. Recall that in 1374 he had already turned his home over to a community of women. Grote himself lived monastically, if you will, after his conversion in 1374. In his *vita* written by Rudolph Dier (d. 1458), Grote is described as someone who lives terribly simply, wearing worn out clothing and eating modestly and sparsely.[14] In Dier's estimation, Grote is a paradigm of humility and poverty. It appears that others found Grote's lifestyle attractive and his preaching persuasive, so much so that they came to him to live in community so as to further themselves in devotion to God. In one place Grote refers to these men as his *socii* (companions) and in another place they are called *spirituales* (spirituals). According to the *vita* of Grote written by Thomas à Kempis, "He had it in mind to build a Monastery for Clerks of the Order of Regular Canons, for he wished to move some of those Clerks who followed him and were fitted for such a life, to take the Religious habit in order that they might serve as an example to other devout persons, and show the way of holiness to any clerks or lay folk that came from elsewhere."[15] Realizing that he was too busy to take leadership over this nascent community, Grote

---

13. Van Zijl, *Gerard Grote*, 161.

14. In one place Dier refers to the humble "habit" (*habitum*) that Grote adopted after his conversion and says that he wore a penitential garment over it and a hair shirt underneath it. See Dumbar, *Reipublicæ daventriensi ab actis: Analecta*, 3.

15. Thomas à Kempis, *Life of Gerard the Great* 15.3; Arthur, trans., *The Founders of the New Devotion*, 45.

appointed one of his confreres, Florentius (Florens) Radewijns (d. 1400), as "father" and "ruler" to the brothers.[16]

Radewijns studied in Prague and then became a canon at St. Peter's, Utrecht. In 1383 he was ordained a priest, likely at the behest of Grote.[17] Coming under Grote's influence, Radewijns "was pricked to the heart," resigning his canonry and taking a poor benefice in Deventer in order to be near Grote.[18] It was in Radewijns vicarage where Grote's followers resided after his death, spending their time copying books and teaching young, poor children who might have a vocation to religious life. Like Grote, Radewijns was known for the simplicity of his clothing, his humility, and his work among the poor, the sick, and the friendless. The community in Deventer began when Radewijns gathered together (probably in 1383), in the words of Dier, "young men of good will."[19] It appears that there were five (perhaps six) men in the initial community, three of whom are named by Dier (including Thomas à Kempis' brother John) along with "some others" (*plures alii*),[20] and not including the young school boys. Hence the beginnings of the Brothers and Sisters of the Common Life.

Though Radewijns' house in Deventer was ground zero for the institutional form of the Brothers and Sisters of the Common Life, John Van Engen has shown that the movement itself in its earliest days was just as much, if not more, theological than institutional. The key theological terms are *conversio* (conversion), *resolutio/intentio*

---

16. Thomas à Kempis, *Life of Gerard the Great* 16.3.

17. The date of Radewijns ordination is debated. I am following Post, *The Modern Devotion*, 202.

18. Thomas à Kempis, *Life of Florentius* 6.2; Arthur, trans., *The Founders of the New Devotion*, 94.

19. Dumbar, *Reipublicæ daventriensi ab actis: Analecta*, 12.

20. Dumbar, *Reipublicæ daventriensi ab actis: Analecta*, 12.

(resolution/intention), and *exercitium* (exercise). When a man or a woman decided to join one of the houses like that at Deventer, it was often referred to as his or her "conversion." In the earliest life of Grote, a rhymed text of 239 lines from 1421, the anonymous author lays out Grote's worldly rise to prestige, but then writes that Grote "converted himself thoroughly, without falsity, without reserve, devoting himself to a hatred as profound as he had hitherto disliked himself."[21] Likewise, Thomas à Kempis in his *vita* writes that "God . . . had decreed to loose this learned and most famous Master from the bonds of this present world, He brought the process of that conversion to full effect."[22]

The concept and language of conversion was not new with the Brothers and Sisters of the Common Life.[23] For example, in the twelfth century, the Cistercian Bernard of Clairvaux (d. 1153) wrote a whole treatise entitled *On Conversion* wherein he said that there is "no true life for us except in conversion, and no other access to a true life."[24] Nonetheless, the language of conversion was the particular currency of discourse for the Brothers and Sisters. When one turned from their worldly ways to the ways of God à la Grote then they experienced a conversion. Those who led others to convert (e.g., Grote's role in converting Radewijns) "by example or preaching were said to have converted them." In fact, their whole way of life, not just the moment of their conversion, was referred to as a *conversio* because everything "began and ended in conversion, in turning the

21. Translation my own. Latin text in Brandsma, "Twee berijmde Levens van Geert Groote," 33.

22. Thomas à Kempis, *Life of Gerard the Great* 3.1; Arthur, trans., *The Founders of the New Devotion*, 8.

23. Van Engen, *Sisters and Brothers of the Common Life*, 14–19.

24. Cited in Van Engen, *Sisters and Brothers of the Common Life*, 14.

The Brothers and Sisters of the Common Life

self toward the Lord."[25] Gerard Zerbolt (d. 1398) went so far as to say that "Truly and spiritually to be converted is to convert, reduce, and reform the affections and powers of the soul . . . to their rightful state."[26] This conversion was necessary because the present state of humankind's condition was one of inconstancy and misery. Humanity was fallen, having lost the peace, happiness, and joy of God.

In the end, what the Brothers and Sisters are doing is returning to an Augustinian understanding of the Christian life. Augustine of Hippo spent a large part of his early adult life fleeing God and pursuing the things of the world—the very kinds of things that Grote spurned upon his conversion. Writing ten years after his "conversion moment" in a garden in Milan, Augustine is able to look back at his life and construct a narrative of it that became a (perhaps *the*) dominant Christian narrative of sin and conversion. Though Augustine's doctrinal works were particularly popular in the Middle Ages and beyond, the *Confessions* were not so well known. They enjoyed an early popularity that died down until the early modern era.[27] Nonetheless, it is hard not to see an Augustinian-like influence, even if it was refracted through the works of others, like Bernard of Clairvaux, on the Brothers and Sisters, especially their conception of conversion. Again, Augustine's narrative of his life and conversion sounds incredibly similar to Grote: "I aspired to honours, money, marriage, and you laughed at me. In those ambitions I suffered the bitterest difficulties; that was by your mercy. . . . Look into my heart, Lord. In obedience to your will I recall this and confess to you. May my soul now adhere to you. . . . How unhappy it was!" And

25. Van Engen, *Devotio moderna*, 28.

26. Gerard Zerbolt de Zutphen, *Manual of Interior Reform* 3; cited in Van Engen, *Sisters and Brothers of the Common Life*, 78.

27. Wills, *Augustine's Confessions: A Biography*, 133–37.

then, just when things seemed beyond hope, "Your scalpel cut to the quick of the wound, so that I should leave all these ambitions and be converted to you, who are 'above all things' (Rom. 9:5) and without whom all things are nothing, and that by conversion I should be healed."[28]

This language of conversion is biblical, of course, likely coming from Psalm 21:28a and Psalm 50:18 in the Vulgate version of the Bible used by Augustine: "All the ends of the earth shall remember, and shall be converted to the Lord," and "I will teach the unjust thy ways: and the wicked shall be converted to thee."[29] Similarly, the prophet Isaiah writes, "Blind the heart of this people, and make their ears heavy, and shut their eyes: lest they see with their eyes, and hear with their ears, and understand with their heart, and be converted and I heal them" (6:10; Douay-Rheims). Augustine's narrative is powerful and persuasive, forming a paradigm of worldly living followed by a dramatic conversion and total reformation of life. Augustine's ultimate conversion to God follows this pattern:

> From a hidden depth a profound self-examination had dredged up a heap of all my misery and set it "in the sight of my heart" (Ps. 18:15). That precipitated a vast storm bearing a massive downpour of tears.... I repeatedly said to [God]: "How long, O Lord? How long, Lord, will you be angry to the uttermost? Do not be mindful of our old iniquities" (Ps. 6:4). For I felt my past to have a grip on me.... As I was saying this and weeping in the bitter agony of my heart, suddenly I heard a voice from the nearby house chanting ... , "Pick up and read, pick up and

---

28. Augustine of Hippo, *Confessions* 6.6.9; Chadwick, trans., *Saint Augustine: Confessions*, 97.

29. Taken from the Douay-Rheims translation of the Vulgate, the Latin edition of the Bible made by Jerome in the early fifth century.

read." . . . I checked the flood of tears and stood up. I interpreted it solely as a divine command to me to open the book [i.e., the Bible] and read the first chapter I might find. For I had heard how Antony [the Great of Egypt] happened to be present at the gospel reading, and took it as an admonition addressed to himself when the words were read: "Go, sell all you have, give to the poor, and you shall have treasure in heaven; and come, follow me" (Matt. 19:21). By such an inspired utterance he was immediately "converted to you" (Ps. 50:15). So I hurried back. . . . There I had put down the apostle when I got up. I seized it, opened it, and in silence read the first passage on which my eyes lit: "Not in riots and drunken parties, not in eroticism and indecencies, not in strife and rivalry, but put on the Lord Jesus Christ and make no provision for the flesh in its lusts" (Rom. 13:13-14). I neither wished nor needed to read further. At once, with the last words of this sentence, it was as if a light of relief from all anxiety flooded into my heart. All the shadows of doubt were dispelled. . . . The effect of your converting me to yourself was that I did not now seek a wife [i.e., he was delivered from his lust for women] and had no ambition for success in this world.[30]

Note the essential ingredients of Augustine's conversion narrative: (i) a highlighting of his sinfulness and his remorse; (ii) the intervention of God (by way of the mysterious voice); (iii) the example of someone else converted to God (i.e., Anthony of Egypt); and (iv) Augustine's immediate and miraculous deliverance from his former way of life and his resolution/intention to now live for God.

30. Augustine of Hippo, *Confessions* 8.11.29-30; Chadwick, trans., *Saint Augustine: Confessions*, 152-53.

Apart from the work of God's grace in the life of a person, resolution/intention "was at the heart of that process of conversion."[31] In the earliest life of Grote quoted above, the author states that Grote "converted himself thoroughly" (*convertit se plenarie*). This use of the reflexive pronoun *se* is not there because the anonymous author thinks that Grote converted himself apart from the grace and work of God. Nonetheless, the author is not conceding that Grote was merely a passive participant in his conversion wherein God did all of the work. The Brothers and Sisters "conceded the need for divine grace and the reality of providential intervention in their lives, and whatever their theological reflections in this regard, their emphasis fell in practice on a personal resolution to change one's status in life and to start down a surer path to salvation."[32] Perhaps the greatest example of this is the aforementioned "Resolutions and Intentions" of Grote. The purpose of these resolutions and intentions was to order his life so that it would be pleasing to God and for the salvation of his soul. Theologically Grote was not converted all at once, as if it was an event that happened in an instantaneous moment. Rather, he sees the rest of his life as part of his conversion, an ongoing process of salvation. Hence, his felt need to lay down his resolutions and intentions. By this action, Grote established for subsequent Brothers and Sisters a pattern that many of them would follow, for not only were Grote's "Resolutions and Intentions" written down and preserved, they were then seen as exemplary, so much so that subsequent followers also wrote down their own resolutions and intentions. This is true especially of those brothers and sisters who did not immediately join a community wherein they were obliged to follow a proper monastic rule, such as the *Rule of Augustine*

31. Van Engen, *Devotio moderna*, 29.
32. Van Engen, *Devotio moderna*, 29.

at Windesheim. In Grote's own understanding, these were resolutions and intentions *not* vows (*non vota*) to be taken and then followed. The ultimate purpose of these intentions and resolutions was to exercise the convert.

"Exercise" for the Brothers and Sisters could be applied to their whole lifestyle or used more frequently to speak of their spiritual theology. It referred to the "spiritual training" to which they submitted themselves, born from their intentions and resolutions. Van Engen explains the extent of what they considered exercises. He writes,

> When they read in Scripture or a devotional book, when they systematically focused on the life and passion of Christ at certain times of the day and attempted to absorb and relive it, all of that counted as "exercising," as training their spiritual selves. The same held for practice in the virtues. When they put themselves out in a matter of obedience, fasted to counteract wicked imaginations, accepted chastisement from a brother or sister without demur, and so on through a long and nearly endless list, this too came under the category of spiritual exercises.[33]

Zerbolt's *The Spiritual Ascent* provides a good example of how a brother incorporated exercises into his spiritual theology. From the outset Zerbolt lays down five points necessary in order to make progress in the spiritual life: 1) set oneself on the place where one will ascend; 2) consider where one begins the ascent (i.e., the "valley of tears"); 3) "carefully review in your heart the means and exercises needed to reach back" in order to recover one's "lost dignity"; 4) request God's help; and 5) remember the "whence, how, and why" for making one's ascent.[34] In short, one who

33. Van Engen, *Devotio moderna*, 29–30.
34. Van Engen, *Devotio moderna*, 245–46.

seeks to grow spiritually needs to remember that he fell away from God through sin and that God has made a way for him to return, through various "means and exercises" and with God's help. And one should make this ascent intentionally so as to be saved and healed.

Concerning these "means and exercises," Zerbolt elaborates, "Before you ascend . . . your heart must be well disposed to reach its end, which is purity of heart and love. Carefully examine and consider what suits you, what is most useful, and if you do not know, ask others, or rather have others order your ascent."[35] Notice the progression: a heart disposed to its proper end leads to an examination of exercises that will be most useful and suitable to *you*. In other words, this is not a "one size fits all" model of spiritual progress and ascent but one that is catered to each believer, just like one's resolutions and intentions are individualized. He continues, "Set a certain end in your heart toward which by grace you may come to complete all your works and exercises. Then order the steps, exercises, and means by which to reach that end, and fix both the end and the means firmly in your heart."[36]

Perhaps a specific example (of my making) will flesh things out. Now that I have a properly disposed heart, I come to see that I need to quit being gluttonous in order to make my ascent to God. So, I set fasting and eating simple food as the "certain end" to which I aspire. I then order my "steps, exercises, and means" to this end by choosing to fast from meat except on church feast days, for example, and to remove all sweet foods from my diet. The exercise happens when I follow through with these resolutions and intentions, which I have likely written down and/or discussed with my spiritual guide. To return to Grote's "Resolutions

---

35. Van Engen, *Devotio moderna*, 255.
36. Van Engen, *Devotio moderna*, 255.

and Intentions," though he desires never to drink wine when healthy (and because it is too expensive!), he would have followed through with the intention by the particular exercises of literally *not* drinking wine. A modern example is this: if I want to get in good physical condition, it is not enough for me to *wish* it; I have to *exercise*. The parallels to the exercises of the Brothers and Sisters is, I hope, obvious. Taken together these Brothers and Sisters undergoing conversion by making intentions and resolutions and carrying them out through exercise were unlike the established monasteries that dominated the spiritual landscape of medieval Europe. Monks and nuns took vows and lived under a formal rule whereas the earliest Brothers and Sisters did not. But in time this would change and these men and women would be formally recognized by the church and others (though not always welcomed) as practitioners of a new kind of devotion.

THE DEVOTIO MODERNA (MODERN DEVOTION)

Between 1415 and 1420, Henry Pomerius, a canon regular of the monastery at Groenendael, was writing a life of the Flemish mystic John Ruusbroec (d. 1381). In this text he records a meeting between Ruusbroec and Grote, claiming that Grote was the "font and origin of the modern devotion in Lower Germany among the Canon Regulars."[37] A decade or more later the prior of Windesheim wrote a short history of the Grote-founded movement in which he titled a section "On the rise of the new devotion in our land."[38] Johannes Busch, mentioned above, writing in the 1460s,

37. Translation my own. Latin text in "De origine monasterii Viridisvallis," 288.

38. Cited in Van Engen, *Devotio moderna*, 7.

also refers to Windesheimians as the Modern Devotion.[39] Thus, only a generation or so after the death of Grote the movement that he "founded" was known as the Modern Devotion. It was a "modern devotion" because they sought to appropriate in their age (*moderna*) the piety (*devotio*) of Christians from earlier days. In one sense, the phrase "Modern Devotion" is just another name for the Brothers and Sisters of the Common Life, but it seems reasonable to make a bit of a distinction between the two, not in thought or spirituality but in organization and institutionalization.

What had begun primarily as a lay movement became, in the end, largely clerical and/or fully monastic. Kasper Elm even went so far as to say that the Brothers and Sisters lived a lifestyle somewhere between "monastery and world."[40] That is, somewhere between a formal monastic life and a converted life outside a cloister. They lived a ruled life without actually living under a *formal* rule, thus they were "semi-religious."[41] As mentioned before, in 1374, just after his conversion, Grote legally turned his ancestral home over to a group of women, keeping a small space in the house for himself. But it is important to see that this was *not* the beginnings of the institutionalization of the movement that would in time be known as the Brothers and

39. Busch, *Chronicon Windeshemense-Liber de Reformatione Monasteriorum*, 251–56.

40. Elm, "Die Brüderschaft vom gemeinsamen Leben."

41. Elm, "*Vita regularis sine regula*." In a somewhat autobiographical though satirical letter written in 1516, Erasmus of Rotterdam (d. 1536), who may have been educated at Deventer by members of the Modern Devotion, refers to his teacher "Florentius" (a made up name) as a "stupid guardian" who, when faced with failure in running a school, "recruited for the last act of his drama a miscellaneous cast of differing social status and even sex, monks, half-monks [*semimonachos*], kinsmen male and female, young and old, known and unknown" (Mynors and Thomson, trans., *The Correspondence of Erasmus*, 15). Elm is using the term more positively and charitably.

Sisters of the Common Life and later the Modern Devotion. As Post notes, "this handing over of his property was by no means the founding of the Sisters of the Common Life. Groote [sic] had as yet no idea of founding a congregation of Sisters who would share table, dormitory, income, and possessions and yet were not bound by the three monastic vows [of poverty, chastity, and obedience]."[42] The nature and purpose of this community is provided in a set of legal statutes drawn up in 1369. Post summarizes the contents of this statute: 1) the house would not serve as the foundation of a new monastic order; 2) it would provide a dwelling place for young women without binding them by vows; 3) if a resident left the community they were not allowed to return; 4) each woman remained a layperson, subject to secular law; 5) the city magistrates would decide who could be admitted to the house; 6) those living in the house would not wear a distinctive habit; 7) no one was to pay a dowry upon entering the house; 8) the women must be careful of making unnecessarily intimate friendships with others in the house; 9) there would be a "mistress" of the house, elected annually on March 12 (the feast of Gregory the Great) by majority vote, and then confirmed by the magistrates; 10) the mistress would make decisions regarding the house and its income and would assign manual labor to members of the house and oversee behavior; 11) everyone had to live by doing manual labor and they were not allowed to beg for their provisions; 12) men were not allowed to visit, stay, or eat in the house; 13) members were expected to be at the house and could not stay elsewhere; and 14) the women needed permission from the magistrates to travel outside the city of Deventer.[43] Post concludes, "These statutes describe the Sisters not as Sisters of the Common Life, but

42. Post, *The Modern Devotion*, 260.
43. Post, *The Modern Devotion*, 262–63.

as almshouse-dwellers."[44] Again, the fully mature (i.e., institutionalized) Brothers and Sisters and Modern Devotion would come later.

The existence and growth of these houses of women was not without controversy. In the high and late Middle Ages (from around 1215) there was a plethora of religious movements involving lay people. Taking a myriad of forms, the church had a difficult time keeping up, if you will. Stated negatively, the church reserved the right to recognize formal groups of men and women who were, in the church's estimation, living as proper religious and monastics, even if these groups did not think of themselves in those terms. Stated positively, the church's hierarchy were keen on ensuring that this wave of religious renewal remained orthodox and within the bounds of proper practice. Every age has its heretical religious fanatics and the Middle Ages was no exception.[45] With the rise of the "profit economy" and the renewal of old Roman roadways that led to more and more people traversing Europe, there was a new market for self-made and self-appointed religious leaders.[46] The church itself recognized this difficulty with the proliferation of new monastic orders towards the late twelfth century and decreed at the Fourth Lateran Council in 1215 that new religious orders needed to adopt an already existing monastic rule, like the *Rule of Augustine* or the *Rule of Benedict*.[47]

---

44. Post, *The Modern Devotion*, 263. Post thinks that it was only in 1398–99 that these women, and other communities like them, became Sisters of the Common Life (see ibid., 265).

45. See, for example Grundmann, *Religious Movements in the Middle Ages*; and Lerner, *The Heresy of the Free Spirit in the Later Middle Ages*.

46. Little, *Religious Poverty and the Profit Economy in Medieval Europe*.

47. Fourth Lateran Council, Canon 13; Tanner, ed., *Decrees of the Ecumenical Councils, Volume I*, 242.

The Brothers and Sisters of the Common Life

Things were further complicated, or made more interesting, with the arrival of the Dominicans and especially the Franciscans, also in the early thirteenth century. With the profit economy came greater mobility and with greater mobility came the rise of cities and urbanism. The Dominicans' and Franciscans' very raison d'être was to minister in this context since they themselves did not live cloistered in one location and they were to beg for their sustenance. In quick time these orders welcomed thousands of new men into their ranks and both also gave birth to a "second order" of women. But their impact on society meant that men and women who did not have religious vocations wanted to formally associate themselves with these orders. Thus, the "third order" was born. Third orders were a common feature of monastic life beginning in the Middle Ages. They were open to persons who desired to have a formal connection to a particular religious order without taking formal vows. The name "third order" comes from the fact that vowed men were seen as the first order; vowed women were the second order; and non-vowed persons constituted the third order, sometimes known as tertiaries. Hence, before long cities were filled with men and women who belonged to these so-called third orders, creating, again, the need for the church to attempt some sort of organizational control. On top of this were the also the aforementioned Beghards and Beguines. Given the prevailing medieval view of salvation, there was a real concern by the church to ensure that those living vowed lives were not collapsed into those who were not.[48] Consequently, if members of the third orders

---

48. In short, the monastic life was seen as superior to non-monastic forms of life and was, therefore, more salvific. Monks and nuns, it was assumed, would spend less time in Purgatory because of their vocation than "normal" men and women, who soiled themselves in life by way of sex, money, etc.

needed to be regulated, how much more so men and especially women like those living in Grote's house.

This influence of the church's hierarchy on lay forms of religious life is evidenced also in the history of the Sisters of the Common Life. Sometime in the 1390s there were a series of attacks made on the Brothers and Sisters by citizens who thought they were not living in community properly. That is, these citizens saw these houses and expected them to be monastic houses, but when they learned that they were not monastic they attacked the houses and those living in them. For this and other reasons, the Brothers and Sisters moved towards being a proper monastic order. In chapter 1, I discussed how the men became Augustinian canons, founding the Windesheim Congregation. The women likewise became Augustinian canonesses, also joining the Windesheim Congregation. In 1392, the city magistrates appointed John Brinckerinck (d. 1419) to oversee the community at Grote's house. Through his effective preaching many women were drawn to the house, but space was limited to only sixteen occupants. Brinckerinck encouraged these women to move to other parts of the city and found new houses. Further, since well-to-do women could not be members of the Grote house community, due to their wealth, he built them a house at Diepenveen in 1400 with statues that allowed women who were not seeking housing due to poverty. The number of houses and members continued to grow so that at Brinckerinck's death there were 150 Sisters living in houses.[49] Their transition from houses of lay women to canonesses is summarized by Post:

> Perhaps because complaints began to be heard concerning these Sisters, who attracted attention by their very numbers, and perhaps too to introduce a little order in the affairs of the Sisterhood,

---

49. Post, *The Modern Devotion*, 269.

> various eminent ecclesiastical persons began to suggest, as early as 1397–98, that these communities of Sisters should adopt an approved monastic order and transform themselves into convents. A considerable campaign was conducted to this end at the end of the fourteenth and the beginning of the fifteenth century, among the Sisters and their spiritual directors. Several Sisters and some of the Brothers were persuaded to accept at least the Third Order of St. Francis. This did not of course immediately transform the Devotionalists into monastics, since people in the world could also adopt this rule, for which the three monastic vows were not required. Yet still the inclination towards the monastic life was there. The community of life, possessions and income and the similarity of the practice of virtue according to a fixed time-table and according to this Third Rule, all these were conducive to it.
>
> An additional factor was that these persons, bound by the rule of St. Francis, soon obtained permission to take the vow of chastity, and gradually the other two vows as well. They even became obligatory for certain groups. By adopting this rule, the Sisters (and Brothers) of the Common Life, gradually and almost imperceptibly, yet according to their own wish, were transformed into monastics. The taking of the vows changed the status of the Brethren and Sisters. A shorter road to transition was the adoption of the rule of St. Augustine.[50]

For example, at a meeting in 1399, a group of leaders of the Brothers met, agreeing that the various Sisters houses that had adopted the Franciscan Third Rule should unite.

50. Post, *The Modern Devotion*, 269–70.

On January 18, 1400, they received a privilege from Pope Boniface IX formally recognizing them and giving them permission to hold an annual chapter and elect a superior-general. Moreover, for those led to do so, they could take a vow of chastity. In 1439, this group had seventy houses and three thousand members. Other houses also joined together, some following the Franciscan model while others, like those that joined the Windesheim Congregation, following the *Rule of Augustine*.[51] Thus, within fifty years of Grote's death, the Brothers and Sisters of the Common Life were thriving as the Modern Devotion.

DISCUSSION QUESTIONS

1. Geert Grote does not recommend monasticism for everyone. What is the difference between monasticism and Grote's "devotionalism"?

2. What elements were key to the structure of the houses of the Brothers and Sisters of the Common Life? What distinguished them from (i) monasticism and (ii) the world?

3. What does the word "conversion" mean in the late medieval context?

4. How can you adopt the practice of Gerard Zerbolt's *Spiritual Ascent*?

---

51. For other examples of houses of men and women becoming properly monastic see Post, *The Modern Devotion*, 273–92; and Van Engen, *Sisters and Brothers of the Common Life*, 119–61.

3

THOMAS HEMERKEN À KEMPIS' LIFE AND FORMATION

EARLY LIFE AND EDUCATION

THOMAS HEMERKEN WAS BORN in Kempen in the Lower Rhine between September 29, 1379 and July 24, 1380 in what is now Germany. His father was a craftsman (probably a blacksmith) and his mother was likely a teacher. His surname, Hemerken, means "little hammer" and was most undoubtedly bestowed on the family as a result of his father's profession. Thomas was initially educated in Kempen but as a teenager, ca. 1393, he studied in Deventer with the Brothers of the Common Life for five or six years. The choice of Deventer seems due to the presence of his brother John in the community there.[1]

---

1. John à Kempis was one of the founding members of the first Brothers of the Common Life community, founded at the behest of Geert Grote under the leadership of Florentius Radewijns. See chapter 2 for details.

THOMAS À KEMPIS

From the start, the Brothers of the Common Life were involved in education. Successful Latin schools were already a common feature in cities like Deventer before the start of the Brothers. Geert Grote himself was in communication with some of these schools after his conversion but before the founding of the Brothers community. In local communities like Kempen, the schools often only provided instruction in reading and writing, hence students had to move elsewhere in order to receive a university preparation-level education, which was often also meant as foundational for a career in the church, especially since they studied philosophy, theology, and Hebrew.[2] Brothers of the Common Life like John and Thomas à Kempis, Gerard Zerbolt, and John Brinckerinck had all moved to Deventer as children to receive their education. Other cities, like Zwolle, also possessed these more advanced schools.

Just as university students had to secure housing when they arrived, these *extranei* (students from outside the city) also had to find housing. Hence, *domus pauperum* (houses for children) or hostels were established in which the boys received assistance with their studies and were often subject to further religious education by way of sermons and collations (edifying talks). Though these types of institutions existed well before the foundation of the Brothers of the Common Life, it is not surprising to see that many of the Brothers communities took in these school children in order to earn income, but also to assist in their education. In time many of the boys in these schools who housed with the Brothers would enter the community themselves as adults. Erasmus of Rotterdam, speaking negatively about the hostel for schoolchildren in 's-Hertogenbosch, reports that the Brothers "exerted heavy pressure on their pupils in order to gain them for the monastic state."[3] In a satiri-

---

2. Laetus, *Belgii confœderati respublica*, 242.
3. Post, *The Modern Devotion*, 254.

cal letter about his own experiences at a Modern Devotion school, Erasmus writes,

> There are two brothers . . . . When quite small, they lost their mother, their father died some time afterwards, leaving a slender estate. . . . The trustees [of their father's estate] had formed the idea of educating them for a monastery. . . . To this the trustees were already inclined, and a certain Warden, a proud man with a great reputation for piety, had pushed them into it, one of them especially who was the schoolmaster under whom the boys in their earliest years had learnt the rudiments of grammar. . . . He seems to be of the same persuasion as many others I have known, thinking that he sacrificed a victim most pleasing to God if he should have consigned one of his pupils to the monastic life, and is wont to recount with pride how many young men every year he had gained for Francis or Dominic or Benedict or Augustine or Bridget.[4]

Post also notes that the superior of the Augustinian canons of the Order of the Holy Cross (i.e., the Croziers) in 1424 affirmed that the Brother's schools had provided numerous members of his order. Further, John Brugman, a Franciscan preacher, wrote in 1471, "The Brothers give to their pupils not scholarship and philosophy but the milk of Christ and thus provided many candidates for priesthood and monastery." Even on the eve of the Reformation, in 1514, the bishop of Utrecht, Frederic von Baden, writes, "the *fraters* [Brothers] have their fruits in various churches and monasteries, for they seclude the schoolboys from the wicked world, educate and preserve them in virtuous ways and in the fear of God and so render them suitable for the religious

4. Erasmus, *Letter 447*; Mynors and Thomson, trans., *The Correspondence of Erasmus*, 10.

houses and churches."⁵ No wonder then that Erasmus would still be saying this in 1516.

Though there is no literary record of Thomas being destined for the monastery by his parents, the example of his brother must have loomed large in his imagination, not much less the example and influence of the Brothers. He arrived in Deventer, it appears, without sufficient funding, which was often the case with young pupils from smaller towns. His brother John, now living in community and with little recourse to money, sent Thomas to Radewijns, who took Thomas into his house (alongside other schoolboys) and provided him with the necessary books. Radewijns then secured a space for Thomas with a local pious woman. In Thomas' own words,

> When I came into the presence of the reverend Father he kept me for a while with him in his house, being moved thereto by fatherly affection; and he placed me in the School, and besides this gave me the books which he thought I needed. Afterwards he obtained for me a lodging, at no cost to myself, with a certain honorable and devout matron.⁶

After some time there he moved into the hostel run by the Brothers, remaining for a year, before moving in with another pious woman and then into a hostel again. When living with the Brothers, Thomas was greatly affected by what he witnessed. He tells us that "being associated with this man [Radewijns] who was so holy, and with the Brothers of his Order, I had their devout lives daily in my mind and before my eyes, and I took pleasure and delight in the contemplation of their godly conduct, and in the gracious

---

5. Post, *The Modern Devotion*, 253–54.

6. Thomas à Kempis, *Life of John Gronde* 1.2; Arthur, trans., *The Founders of the New Devotion*, 170.

words which proceeded from the mouths of these humble men. Never before could I recollect to have seen such men, so devout and fervent were they in the love of God and of their neighbor."[7] It is not surprising then that when Thomas finished his education he, having witnessed such exemplars of the religious life, would, in 1399, enter the community of the regular canons at Mt. St. Agnes near Zwolle.

LIFE AS AN AUGUSTINIAN CANON

In 1384, on the recommendation of Grote, a group of Brothers settled on what was then called Nemelerberg (Mt. Nemel).[8] The house became a monastery during the early wave of institutionalism in 1398 and John à Kempis was appointed its first prior.[9] The history of the community is known because of Thomas' own *Chronicle of the Canons Regular of Mount St. Agnes*. Recounting the founding of the community, Thomas writes,

> Now there were in the State of Zwolle certain faithful men who had been turned wholly to God by Master Gerard Groote [*sic*]. . . . And as these servants of God lived in poverty and at the common charge it came to pass that many men that were in the world, considering their holy life, came together to them, being eager to serve God and to leave the world, in the hope of an eternal gain. Meanwhile it happened that the venerable Master Gerard Groote came to Zwolle about the beginning of Lent. . . . When the most beloved Master was sojourning in Zwolle for the

---

7. Thomas à Kempis, *Life of John Gronde* 1.2; Arthur, trans., *The Founders of the New Devotion*, 170.

8. Though the community's founding document only dates from 1395.

9. Because of the Reformation the house was abolished in 1561 and the community disbanded in 1581.

purpose of preaching the Word, some of his disciples aforementioned who dwelt together there came to him secretly and confessed that they desired to live a life further removed from that of the world, for they could not bear to mingle with worldlings without suffering hurt to their spiritual life; and they said that they would choose to dwell without the City if he should agree thereto. They begged him therefore, as loving sons speaking to their father, to condescend to go with them some little space outside the City to look for a place convenient wherein to live quietly. Then Gerard assented to their pious prayers.[10]

Surveying locations around Zwolle, Grote chose for them a place that provided level ground so that they would be able to grow their own crops and be self-sustaining. Though he expressed a desire to join them, Grote died the same year, never seeing the first house that they built.

Though Thomas entered the community the next year (1399), he did not make final profession until 1407. The length of his formation is unusual, though it is possibly due to the house's poverty in its first years and, thereby, its instability.[11] Nikolaus Staubach writes that Thomas entered as a *donatus* in 1399, only being invested as a novice in 1406, taking his final vows the following year.[12] This view goes back to 1880, when O. A. Spitzen published his work on the

10. Thomas à Kempis, *Chronicle* 1; Arthur, trans., *The Chronicle of the Canons*, 1–6.

11. Cf. Thomas à Kempis, *Chronicle* 2.

12. Staubach, "Thomas à Kempis," 690. A *donatus* is someone who has given himself to a religious community but is not a vowed member of that community. Thus, there is a formal connection between the person and the community but not necessarily a life-long commitment.

Imitation of Christ.¹³ The view was made even more known two years later when Victor Becker repeated Spitzen's "true explanation" and also asserted that Thomas was received "as a *donatus* and lived there [at Mt. St. Agnes] for a few years in this capacity."¹⁴ Becker thinks that it is clear that Thomas was a *donatus* based on Thomas' own language in the *Chronicle*. Thomas says that he came earnestly "to the house" (*pro mansion*) and was "accepted" (*acceptatus*). Becker concludes, "This expression *pro mansione* is very suitable for someone who, although not a religious [i.e., monk], wants to remain in the monastery, but it does not suit a religious. The word *acceptatus* was also the usual term to express the admission of *donati*."¹⁵ Based on the constitutions of Windesheim, which now governed Mt. St. Agnes as the mother house of the congregation, Becker explains that two biological brothers could not enter the same monastery without three quarters of the canons consenting to it by vote at a chapter meeting and without the consent of the whole General Chapter, made up of the heads of all the houses in the congregation. Thus, thinks Becker, "Thomas indicates quite clearly that he was received as a *donatus*."¹⁶ Becker ultimately concludes, "After having read what Mr. Spitzen has written on this point, I think I can demonstrate, by authentic dates, that Thomas, in presenting himself at Mont-S.-Agnès [*sic*], could not have had the intention of being received among the religious."¹⁷

13. Spitzen, *Thomas a Kempis*.

14. Becker, *L'auteur de l'Imitation et les documents Néerlandais*, 4; my translation.

15. Becker, *L'auteur de l'Imitation et les documents Néerlandais*, 5; my translation.

16. Becker, *L'auteur de l'Imitation et les documents Néerlandais*, 5; my translation.

17. Becker, *L'auteur de l'Imitation et les documents Néerlandais*, 5; my translation. Aug. J. Thebaud concludes that Becker "proves from

In any case, Thomas' long contact with the community, as either a novice or a *donatus*, made him more than ready to take final vows. Writing as a supposedly detached chronicler, Thomas simply says of his investiture as a novice, "In the year of the Lord 1406, on the Feast of Corpus Christi, . . . two brothers that were Clerks, and one that was a Convert, were invested. These were Thomas Hemerken of the city of Kempen . . . [and] Oetbert Wilde of Zwolle."[18] Regarding his final profession he says nothing. He was ordained priest between July 26, 1413 and July 24, 1414. Almost without exception, Thomas spent the remainder of his life at Mt. St. Agnes, primarily writing and copying books and on two occasions (from 1425–31 and in 1448) serving as sub-prior.[19] As a priest he also would have regularly offered Mass and participated in the full liturgical *horarium* of the community. Further, he served as novice master, resulting in a series of talks for novices arranged as a dialogue.[20] He died in 1471 "Having obtained a ripe old age." A later entry into the Mt. St. Agnes Chronicle, not written by Thomas, says, "Brother Thomas was afflicted with dropsy of

---

Thomas himself that he entered as a *donatus* in 1399" (Thebaud, "Who Wrote the 'Imitation of Christ'?" 662); and Albert Ampe states it as fact without additional comment (Ampe, *L'Imitation de Jésus-Christ et son auteur*, 43).

18. Thomas à Kempis, *Chronicle* 10; Arthur, trans., *The Chronicle of the Canons*, 41.

19. In his *Epitaphium monachorum* Thomas writes, "What, O monk, do you do in your cell? I read, I write, I collect honey. This brings solace to my soul. Well said. Indeed, the cell of the monk at work and the study of books ought to be ablaze" (O monache quid facis in cella? Lego scribe colligo mella. Haec animae meae solacia. Bene dixisti. Nam cella monachorum in labore et studio librorum flagere debet). Latin text in Pohl, *Thomae Hemerken a Kempis: Opera omnia, Volume 4*, 143; my translation.

20. Thomas à Kempis, *Sermons to the Novices Regular*.

the limbs, slept in the Lord in the year 1471, and was buried in the East side of the Cloister."[21]

Thomas' literary output is vast, though there are still texts attributed to him that are disputed by scholars today.[22] Speaking to his voluminous output, E. Assemaine, a twentieth-century Benedictine and translator of Thomas, wrote, "The life lived in the monasteries of the Windesheim congregation was very similar to the life we live in Benedictine communities; it was the laborious and not at all monotonous uniformity of a religious house devoted to prayer, study, and work."[23] Thomas says as much himself when he writes in *The Life of the Good Monk*, "Imitate St. Benedict: keep every word spoken to you. It is good to work with your hands."[24] Such laborious monotony gave Thomas the space, time, and rhythm of life to write for the benefit of his community and the church. Characterizing his oeuvre, Staubach concludes that Thomas' works "vary in genre and extent, but in their general subject matter and function they can all be categorized as ascetic and spiritual *exercita devote* ('devotional exercises')."[25] The Carthusian prior of Nuremburg George Pirkamer, writing to the humanist Peter

21. Cited in Cruise, *Thomas a Kempis*, 139.

22. Thomas' works began to be published only three years after his death (see Hellinga, "Thomas à Kempis—the First Printed Editions"), with the first "collected edition" appearing in 1494 (Thomas a Kempis, *Opera et libri vite*). The modern critical edition by Pohl includes thirty-eight works, described in Van Dijk, "Thomas Hemerken a Kempis," 818–21.

23. Cited in Mercier, "Thomas a Kempis," 761; my translation.

24. Thomas à Kempis, *Vita boni monachi* 6; my translation. Latin text in Pohl, *Thomae Hemerken a Kempis: Opera omnia, Volume 4*, 157: "Imitare sanctum Benedictum:
    serva omne verbum tibi dictum.
    Bonum est laborare minibus . . ."

25. Staubach, "Thomas à Kempis," 690.

Dannhäuser, famously stated, "Nothing more holy, nothing more honorable, nothing more religious, nothing in fine more profitable for the Christian commonwealth can you ever do than to make known these works of Thomas à Kempis."[26] The most famous and well-known, of course, is the *Imitation of Christ*, which was securely attributed to Thomas in the twentieth century (see chapter 4). Likely begun by Thomas in his mid-40s, the *Imitation* is a mature presentation of Thomas' understanding of what it means to imitate Jesus as a fully formed devout convert.

THE FORMATION OF THOMAS À KEMPIS

As mentioned above, Thomas was first and foremost a monk. The bulk of his days were spent praying the daily office, saying and/or attending Mass, serving the community through manual labor (e.g., copying manuscripts and, in Thomas' case, writing original works) and, as a canon regular, serving the church sacramentally and ministerially. Yet, what made Thomas (and the other canons) fit for the monastic life was not their intelligence or industry but because they were

> constant in their purpose, and perfectly renounced the pomps of the world by the casting aside of worldly garments, by the exercise of toil and humiliation, by ready submission to all commands and hardships, by mortification of their own will and opinion, by observance of silence and quiet, by zeal in sacred reading and prayer, by the grateful acceptance of blame and correction, by cheerfulness in the watchings and fasts, by readiness to confess their sins, and to disclose their temptations, and all other the like

---

26. Thomas à Kempis, *Opera et libri vite*, f. 3.

> wherein they can be proved, whether they truly will to die to the world and themselves and live to God in the perfection of holy Religion.[27]

Or, to use the language of Grote and the Brothers and Sisters of the Common Life, Thomas made a good monk, fit for the monastery because he was a convert, and a devout one at that. As the Augustinian canon Jordan of Quedlinburg (d. 1380) said in his mid-fourteenth century *Liber Vitasfratrum* (*Book of the Lives of the Brothers*), "the habit does not make the monk, but profession and regular observance."[28] In other words, it is not merely the taking of the habit and making vows that formed Thomas into a regular canon but it was his formation in the monastic life begun as a novice.

In his own talks to novices we can assume that Thomas was saying things similar to what he heard as a novice. That is, we can get a glimpse of his own formation if we look at his sermons to the novices at Mt. St. Agnes. As assembled in book form, the collection begins on an Augustinian note: "Behold, how good and pleasant it is when brothers dwell in unity!"[29] Augustinian because, in the hands of Augustine of Hippo, Psalm 132/133 was a discourse on the monastic life.[30] Composed over a twenty-five year period, Augustine's *Ennarrationes in Psalmos* (*Running Explanations on the Psalms*) comment on all 150 psalms. For Psalm 132/133 Augustine takes the whole scope of salvation history and, in essence, makes it about monastic history.[31] He emphasizes

---

27. *Constitutiones Canonicorum Regularium Capituli Windeshemensis*; cited in Scully, trans., *Sermons to the Novices Regular*, xv.

28. Saak, *High Way to Heaven*, 219, fn. 216; my translation.

29. Psalm 133:1 in modern reckoning but 132:1 in the Latin Vulgate, Thomas' Bible.

30. See Verheijen, "L'*Enarratio in Psalmum* 132 de saint Augustin et sa conception du monachisme."

31. Peters, *The Monkhood of All Believers*, 27–29.

that the whole point of the monastic life is to live together as one, like the earliest Christians as recorded in Acts 2:45 and 4:32. Monks do not just live together, but they live together *as one*. Thus, for Thomas "there is no greater happiness in a monastery of religious and a community of Brothers and Sisters: than unanimity of soul, and concord in virtue with observance of the rule and the statutes: according to the precepts of the superiors, and the counsel of elders." Though Satan attempts to attack the monks, the "united community of brethren struggles and triumphs" by nightly vigil, toil in labor, sacred reading, and devout prayers.[32] Any monk in the community who is not united to the others is cast out for a "convent of monks is like the salt sea, which cannot retain within it dead bodies: but at once casts up on shore what is corrupt, but nourishes what is healthy and fresh, . . . bringing it to perfection." Similarly, "In a community of the Devout the hearts of many are tried, as gold in a burning furnace: whether their desires are of God, or conceived of the flesh."[33]

It appears that for Thomas the religious life will be one of warring with Satan, and the key to winning is, at least in part, to remain constant and vigilant. Life, in general, tempts all men and women with desires of the flesh and fleeting honors. But for the monk, God has prepared their vocation so that in the monastery they are dead to the world, which does not mean that they are not tempted. Rather, the monastery is the ideal battle ground in which to "struggle daily against passions and vices."[34] For the monks

---

32. Thomas à Kempis, *Sermons to the Novices* 1; Scully, trans., *Sermons to the Novices Regular*, 8.

33. Thomas à Kempis, *Sermons to the Novices* 1; Scully, trans., *Sermons to the Novices Regular*, 11.

34. Thomas à Kempis, *Sermons to the Novices* 11; Scully, trans., *Sermons to the Novices Regular*, 64.

are martyrs if they "stand in religion under obedience" and "faithfully fulfill what [they] have vowed."[35] Nonetheless, they must stand not just once but all the time, persevering in the state of religion. Thomas exhorts the novices to "Purpose firmly in your hearts that you desire to remain with constancy in this place and Order which you have freely chosen.... For you have not been called to this community because of your merits: but you should believe that you are made partakers of their [i.e., the martyr's] crowns."[36] Ultimately Thomas concludes,

> Brothers, we are all one in Christ, we have one heavenly Father: we are all called the sons of one holy mother Church, whoever believes in Christ and are baptized in Christ: therefore we ought not to dispute about the outward habit, and different manner of life; but let each study to live well in his Order and condition: and wholly to please God worthily with giving of thanks.[37]

In short, for Thomas, the monastery is the crucible and forge of formation. Nevertheless, Thomas also advocated for the spiritual growth of all Christians, including non-monastics. For Thomas, all devoutly converted believers are to imitate Christ Jesus.

In the *Imitation*, Thomas plainly states what Jordan of Quedlinburg had already said, that the "habit and tonsure by themselves are of small significance; it is the transformation

---

35. Thomas à Kempis, *Sermons to the Novices* 11; Scully, trans., *Sermons to the Novices Regular*, 65. Similarly, "Every one [sic] in the Order living religiously and devoutly in his state, can gain the palm of martyrdom" (Scully, trans., *Sermons to the Novices Regular*, 67).

36. Thomas à Kempis, *Sermons to the Novices* 14; Scully, trans., *Sermons to the Novices Regular*, 83.

37. Thomas à Kempis, *Sermons to the Novices* 14; Scully, trans., *Sermons to the Novices Regular*, 90.

of one's way of life and the complete mortification of the passions that make a true Religious" (1.17; 45). Such a sentiment creates the space necessary for Thomas to affirm non-monastics in their own life of conversion and devotion. As Giles Constable states,

> The third and fourth books [of Thomas' *Imitation*] are in the form of a dialogue between Christ and a disciple. These parts were apparently addressed primarily to priests, since Christ instructed the disciple to examine his conscience and to confess before celebrating holy communion (IV.7.1) and the disciple referred to the pious desires and needs of those "who desire and ask for prayers and masses to be said by me for them and all of theirs" (IV.9.5); but the message of withdrawal, self-conquest and examination, and sanctification of self to God was applicable to all Christians.[38]

Though Thomas was a canon regular and an unapologetic promoter of monasticism, he did not think that those outside the cloister were by necessity damned or somehow less Christian than monks and nuns. As seen above, he does think that the monastery provides a safer space, if you will, to do battle with Satan and he, like most late medieval spiritual authors, is suspicious of "the world." For throughout Christian history there is always a tension between the "world" (*saeculum*) and that which is "spiritual" (*spiritualis*).[39] At times, this results in a loss of the theological understanding

---

38. Constable, *Three Studies in Medieval Religious and Social Thought*, 241.

39. Thomas himself wrote a rhymed and versified work entitled *Vita boni monachi* (*The Life of the Good Monk*) in which he explains how a monk needs to be detached from the world in order to receive the reward of being a true monk. See Van Dijk, "Thomas Hemerken a Kempis," 820:

that God created the world and it was "good" (cf. Gen 1) and gives rise to the worst of the *fuga mundi* (flee the world) tradition. Thomas, fortunately, retains a proper balance in his advocacy of rejecting worldly things while not denigrating it unnecessarily.[40]

Right from the start, in the first chapter of Book 1, which is entitled "Of the Imitation of Christ, and Contempt for all the Vanities of the World," Thomas writes, "it is the highest wisdom, by contempt of the world to press forward toward the kingdom of Heaven."[41] It is foolish and vain to be enslaved to the body, crave possessions, desire a long life, and care only for this life, not for the life to come. Everyone, monk and non-monastic alike, must continually "endeavor to withdraw" their "heart from the love of 'the things that are seen:' and to turn it wholly to 'the things that are not seen.'"[42] And it is this kind of lifestyle that Thomas promotes throughout the *Imitation*, whose impact on early modern spirituality, both inside and outside the monastery, should not be overestimated.

Monache ad quid venisti;	Monk, why are you here;
quare mundum reliquisti?	why have you left the world?
Cur cappam istam induisti;	Why have you put on the cassock;
et pompam mundi despexisti?	and despise worldly ostentation?
Nonne ut Deo servires;	Was it not so you would serve God;
et cor tuum custodires?	and guard your heart?
Cur ergo sic vagaris;	Why, then, do you wander;
et vana meditaris?	and meditate on vain things?
Multum peccas evagando:	Many stray toward sin:
tempus perdis otiando.	time destroys *otium* (tranquility).

40. See Magill, "Turn Away the World," 44–46.

41. Thomas à Kempis, *The Imitation of Christ* 1.1; Payne, trans., *The Imitation of Christ*, 49.

42. Thomas à Kempis, *The Imitation of Christ* 1.1; Payne, trans., *The Imitation of Christ*, 49.

DISCUSSION QUESTIONS

1. What aspects of Thomas à Kempis' upbringing shaped him to be the type of monk he was?
2. How does Augustine's view of "oneness" correspond to the monastery as the ideal battleground in which to "struggle daily against passions and vices"?
3. How does Thomas balance the concept of monasteries being a battleground and the concept of not fleeing from the world?
4. What about Thomas's mission resonates with you?

4

THOMAS' SPIRITUAL THEOLOGY I

The Imitation of Christ

HISTORY OF THE IMITATION OF CHRIST

FOR NEARLY FOUR CENTURIES there was an ongoing debate regarding the authorship of the *Imitation of Christ*. From the start, the text was attributed to a number of medieval authors, including Geert Grote, Jean Gerson (d. 1429), (Pseudo-)Bonaventure, the Carthusian Ludolph of Saxony (d. 1378), and even the Cistercian Bernard of Clairvaux (d. 1153).[1] Sorting out its true authorship was not fully resolved until the mid-twentieth century when, in 1957, Jacques Huijben and Pierre Debongnie were able to declare, "That said, it's the *Imitation*, it's Thomas à Kempis, the only author."[2] It would seem that the autograph (i.e., original)

---

1. For a list of other contenders, see Creasy, *The Imitation of Christ*, xvii.

2. Huijben and Debongnie, *L'auteur our les auteurs de l'Imitation*,

manuscript of the *Imitation*, dating to 1441, thirty years before Thomas' death, would settle the matter.[3] There, on the last page, we read, "Finitus et completus anno Domini m. cccc. xli. per manus fratris Thome Kempis in monte sancte Agnetis prope Zwollis" ("Finished and completed in the year of our Lord 1441 by the hand of brother Thomas of Kampen of Mt. St. Agnes near Zwolle").[4] The problem, however, lies in the phrase "per manus fratris Thome Kempis" ("by the hand of brother Thomas of Kampen"), which could mean that Thomas *authored* the works in the manuscript or that he was the *copyist* of the works in the manuscript. For let us not forget that as much as Thomas was an original author he was also a copyist, as were most of the Brothers in the Windesheim Congregation.[5] Did Thomas write the works in the manuscript or did he just copy the works?

The notion that the *Imitation* might be the work of Gerson, the chancellor of the University of Paris from 1395 to 1429, dates to a 1483 edition of the *Imitation* published in Venice. This attribution is repeated on almost fifty other printed editions prior to 1500, but by the eighteenth century these attributions "all but disappear."[6] The main argument against Gerson's authorship is that despite a number of lists enumerating his works, including several from Gerson himself, none of them ever mention the *Imitation*. Grote's supposed authorship was adamantly argued for by Jacob

---

383: "Cela, c'est l'*Imitation*, c'est Thomas a Kempis, unique auteur."

3. Book 1 of the *Imitation* was completed by 1424, and all four books were done by 1427. Huijben and Debongnie, *L'auteur our les auteurs de l'Imitation*, 3–7.

4. Van den Gheyn, *Catalogue des Manuscrits*, 337.

5. Creasy, *The Imitation of Christ*, xx.

6. Creasy, *The Imitation of Christ*, xvii–xviii. See also Lovatt, "The *Imitation of Christ* in Late Medieval England," 98. Note also that this early plethora of editions demonstrates the immediate popularity of the *Imitation*.

van Ginneken, beginning in 1924, though the thesis seems to no longer have credibility among scholars of the *Imitation*.[7] All other possible authors have been dismissed so that Creasy concludes, "suggesting a high degree of probability is the best we can do: Thomas à Kempis *probably* wrote the *Imitation of Christ*."[8]

Despite uncertainly about the text's author in its earliest years, it has become one of the most copied, printed, and translated books in Christian history. There are nearly eight hundred medieval manuscripts and about 2,300 pre-1800 Latin and vernacular translations of the *Imitation*.[9] In short, the *Imitation* has been read and greatly appreciated by its readers for centuries. At essence, the work is intimate and relatable. Its contents are pertinent to all believers and have resonated through the centuries with myriad of myriads of devout converts. In English, a translation was first made in the second half of the fifteenth century, likely by a Carthusian monk, but this translation remained in manuscript form and only four copies exist today.[10] A much more successful translation was made in 1502 by William Atkinson (d. 1509), a prebend of Southwell near Nottingham, and published in 1503. It was this translation that was aimed at the general public and made the *Imitation* a household name, if you will. So much so that in 1531/32 Thomas More (d. 1535), lawyer, statesman, humanist, and martyr, could write in the preface of his *Confutation of Tyndale's Answer* that "unlearned" people should, "beside their other business in prayer and meditation," read "such English books as most may nourish and increase devotion. Of which kind is

7. Creasy, *The Imitation of Christ*, xviii–xix.

8. Creasy, *The Imitation of Christ*, xx–xxi; italics in the original.

9. Staubach, "Thomas à Kempis," 690.

10. Lovatt, "The *Imitation of Christ* in Late Medieval England," 111; and Creasy, *The Imitation of Christ*, xx–xxi.

Bonaventure's *Of the Life of Christ*, Gerson's *Of the Following of Christ* and the devout contemplative book of *Scala perfectionis* [i.e., Walter Hilton's *Scale of Perfection*] with other such like."[11] Despite More's misattribution of the *Imitation* to Gerson, it is still important to note that he commends the book to all English Christians who are serious about their faith and devotion. More's commendation remains relevant today.

FRAMING THE IMITATION OF CHRIST

There is no secret key that unlocks the spiritual theology of the *Imitation*, but scholars have proposed various ways of approaching the text. For example, Rudolph van Dijk describes the work as "a thematically arranged corpus of aphorisms and sayings," rightfully noting that the autograph manuscript of the *Imitation* (i.e., the one written in/by Thomas' own hand) reverses the traditional printed order of Books 3 and 4.[12] He concludes,

> This original order reflects an overall concept guiding the spiritual journey of Christian believers. Within this concept, dialogue fulfills a central and gradually ascending role. First, *man* (Book I) is addressed by a spiritual mentor (the author) as a *person* (Book II), after that by the Eucharistic [sic] Christ, stimulating him to join Him in conversation as *disciple* (Book III, usually IV) and finally to get involved by Him as *son* (Book IV, usually III) with the eternal, innerdivine conversation of the Trinity.[13]

---

11. Cited in Lovatt, "The *Imitation of Christ* in Late Medieval England," 97; modernized.

12. Van Dijk, "'Sprich Du zu mir, Du einziger,'" 385; my translation.

13. Van Dijk, "'Sprich Du zu mir, Du einziger,'" 385; my translation.

Thomas' Spiritual Theology I

Van Dijk develops this thesis in greater detail elsewhere, noting that by moving Thomas' treatment of the blessed sacrament to the end of the work it "betrays a different concept of the spiritual path than was intended by Thomas."[14] If the *Imitation* ends with a treatment of the Eucharist then it communicates that Thomas' idea of spiritual growth is as follows: spiritualization leads to internalization resulting in consolation, which brings one to a personal relationship with Christ in the Eucharist. That, van Dijk argues, was *not* Thomas' plan but is the result of later editors, copyists, and printers. Van Dijk concludes that it is best to use the order of books as they are given in the autograph manuscript, placing Thomas' treatment of the Eucharist as Book 3. This allows him to conclude that Book 1 discusses humankind in general whereas Book 2 is addressed to readers or listeners as individuals. In Book 3 (modern Book 4) these hearers and listeners become disciples of Jesus Christ and in Book 4 (modern Book 3) they are true sons and daughters of God. Content-wise, van Dijk sees the progression this way: followers of Christ make progress only inasmuch as they internalize his teachings, which leads them to find the kingdom of God within themselves though they can only enter it through trials. Having found the kingdom of God, these believers, urged on by Christ, offer him a dwelling place within themselves by way of the Holy Eucharist that then brings about inner consolation.

Anton Weiler, who also prefers the autograph manuscript ordering of the books, sees great significance in Thomas' use of the language of interiority, which Weiler defines as "the presence of the Divine Word in man [*sic*]."[15] Weiler thinks that interiority is the "all supporting basis of the *Imitatio*" and that its root lies in Thomas' use

14. Van Dijk, "De Structuur van de *Navolging*," 37; my translation.
15. Weiler, "Word from the Beginning," 427.

of Johannine theology.[16] The Gospel of John contains two texts that garner Thomas' notice vis-à-vis interiority: "In the beginning was the Word [*principio erat Verbum*]" (1:1); and "So they said to him, 'Who are you?' Jesus said to them, 'Just what I have been telling you from the beginning' [*principium quia et loquor vobis*]" (8:25). Thomas theologizes on these texts when he writes,

> Those to whom the Eternal Word speaks [*verbum loquitur*] are delivered from uncertainty. From one Word [*verbo*] proceeds all things, and all things tell [*loquuntur*] of Him; it is He, the Author [*principium* = the Beginning] of all things, who speaks to us. Without Him no one can understand or judge aright. But the man [sic] to whom all things are one, who refers everything to One, and who sees everything as in One, is enabled to remain steadfast in heart, and abide at peace with God. (1.3; 30)

Weiler summarizes this as, "Thomas directs man [sic] to his inner self. Man must be one with himself, inwardly simple. A good, inner man hears what the Lord is saying within him."[17] And, "the fundament of Thomas' *Imitatio* is the religious doctrine that God has expressed Himself in his Word 'in the beginning', *in principio*. Men [sic] are created in this Word. . . . The foundation of our existence is the Divine Word, that speaks to us 'from the beginning', and in our inner self calls us 'to be holy and immaculate before his face, in love.'"[18] Thus, it is the concept of interiority that is the main glue that holds the *Imitation* together because the Word is "Present in us, as the *principium* of our existence, He talks to us, and calls us to the unity of love with Him.

---

16. Weiler, "Word from the Beginning," 427.
17. Weiler, "Word from the Beginning," 428.
18. Weiler, "Word from the Beginning," 439.

... Docility and abandoning our limited self must be our God-given answer to the inviting Word, that speaks to us 'from the Beginning.'"[19]

Though the approaches of both van Dijk and Weiler are commendable, neither is preferred above the other. Again, there is not a particular key that unlocks the spiritual theology of the *Imitation*. It seems wise, however, to accept the order of books as they are given in the autograph manuscript. Thus, all references from this point on to Book 3 are to the "Devout Exhortation on the Blessed Sacrament" and Book 4 refers to the "Book on Inward Consolation." With Weiler, the notion of interiority will remain important but it will not serve as the "key" to Thomas' spiritual theology. With van Dijk, I will examine the *Imitation* as a progression of theological-spiritual concepts, though I will not follow his iteration verbatim. I opt instead for the more classical framing of the threefold progression of the spiritual life as a heuristic for reading the *Imitation*.

THE THREEFOLD WAY

Around the year 1200 "the practice of theology emancipated itself from a system of Scripture readings and opted for a conceptual framework derived from philosophy. Parallel to these processes, spirituality too began to systematize itself and to develop its own conceptual patterns around such basic modern categories as affectivity and experience."[20] Evidence for this systematization is found in the tripartite division of the spiritual life: beginner, advanced, and perfected. The earliest proponents of this tripartite scheme are Clement of Alexandria (d. 214) and Origen of Alexandria (d. 254). In Clement, the goal of the spiritual life is the

19. Weiler, "Word from the Beginning," 440.
20. Waaijman, *Spirituality*, 369.

vision of God, which comes by way of knowledge and the practice of love, evidenced in ethical activity. Origen, in his *Commentary on the Song of Songs*, says that Proverbs, Ecclesiastes, and the Song of Songs correspond to three stages of the spiritual life: ethical activity (Proverbs), contemplation of God's creation (Ecclesiastes), and contemplation of the divine being (Song of Songs).[21] Origen's disciple and popularizer of the tripartite division was the monk Evagrius of Pontus (d. 399). The triple way is laid out clearly in his spiritual trilogy: *Praktikos*, *Gnostikos*, and *Kephalaia Gnostica*. First, one eradicates evil by acquiring the virtues through grace and discipline. In the second stage, contemplation of the physical world, one contemplates the physical creation and then moves on to contemplate the spiritual creation of heaven. One can then move to the third stage—contemplation of the Holy Trinity.[22]

This tripartite division initially came into the Latin church through John Cassian (d. ca. 432), Evagrius' disciple. He then influenced, for example, the monk and pope Gregory the Great (d. 604), who, in his *Moralia on Job*, wrote about the "stages of earned merits" one ascends before perfection: "every chosen one first begins with a fragile initiation and later strengthens himself for greater and harder challenges."[23] Centuries later Bernard of Clairvaux employs the triple way in his *Steps of Humility and Pride*: "Beginners are not able to enjoy the sweetness of milk until they have been purged by the bitter draught of fear. It must cleanse them of the infection of carnal pleasures. The perfect now turn from milk since they have had a glorious foretaste of the feast of glory. Only those in the middle, those who are

---

21. Tyler, "Triple Way," 626.

22. See Peters, "Evagrius of Pontus (c346–399)."

23. Gregory the Great, *Moralia on Job* 22.20; Kerns, trans., *Gregory the Great*, 367.

growing, who are still delicate, are content with the sweet milkfoods of charity."[24]

In the high Middle Ages, this tripartite way of beginners, advanced, and perfected took a definitive turn in *The Triple Way* of the Franciscan theologian Bonaventure (d. 1274). This "triple way," says Bonaventure, was laid out by the sixth-century mystical theologian Pseudo-Dionysius to describe the spiritual life's progress: purgation, illumination, and perfection. In Bonaventure, this triple way orders the human soul to its proper actions and to its fitting *telos* (goal/end): union with God. Purgation leads to peace and an upright life through purification from sin. Illumination attends to truth and the imitation of Christ. Perfection, through love, prepares the believer to receive Jesus Christ as Spouse. In purgation the believer is cleansed, aided by spiritual exercises and ascetic practices. Meditation, prayer, and contemplation lead to further advancement. The illuminative way is characterized by further meditation, prayer, and contemplation; reception of the gifts of the Holy Spirit; additional spiritual exercises and devotion to the Virgin Mary. Exercising proper Christian love as one experiences mystical union with God as Trinity distinguishes the unitive way. The purgative and illuminative ways involve the activity of the soul whereas the unitive way is passive while one awaits God's imputation of grace.

This tripartite way became pervasive in Christian spiritual writing, proving "to be so powerful that it absorbed the other triad (beginners, advanced, perfect). This produces a remarkable duplication: the way of purification for beginners, the way of illumination for the advanced, and the way of union for the perfect."[25] This schema retained its place in

---

24. Bernard of Clairvaux, *The Steps of Humility and Pride* 2.4; Conway and Walton, trans., *Bernard of Clairvaux*, 33.

25. Waaijman, *Spirituality*, 375–76.

the writings of the greatest Catholic Reformation spiritual authors of the sixteenth century, such as Ignatius of Loyola (d. 1556), John of the Cross (d. 1591), and Teresa of Avila (d. 1582), and remains popular today. Though there is no definitive evidence that Thomas used this schema explicitly, its ubiquity in medieval spiritual writings gives it, I suggest, pride of place as a heuristic tool. It may also be worth recalling that the *Imitation* was attributed to Bonaventure in some manuscripts. Hence, it has a Bonaventurean ethos and Bonaventure, as noted above, subscribed to the triple way. Finally, such an approach is not unknown in studies of Thomas à Kempis:

> From the time of [Pseudo-]Dionysius the Areopagite mystical writers divided the spiritual life into three stages: Purgation, Illumination, and Consummation. The first two treatises [of the *Imitation*] deal upon the whole with that moral and spiritual discipline without which no man can be a true follower of Christ; the third, on the Sacrament, points to the Eucharist as the means of union with Him who is the Light of the world; the fourth, of Internal Consolation, tells of the presence of Christ in the soul, of life in the spirit, of the mystic vision, as a Kempis [*sic*] understood it.[26]

Nonetheless, this tripartite lens does not equate to a one-to-one correspondence between Thomas' Book 1 and purgation, for example. Each of the three ways are found dispersed throughout the whole *Imitation*.

---

26. Bigg, trans., *The Imitation of Christ*, 5–6.

PURGATION

Purgation from sin can only begin once a believer or, in Thomas' language, a devout person acknowledges her sinful state. For Thomas human nature is corrupted and defective. In fact, the human body itself greatly hinders the "inner life." Thomas writes, "to eat and drink, to wake and sleep, to rest and labour, and to be subject to all the necessities of nature is a great trouble and affliction to the devout man, who would rather be released and set free from all sin" (1.22; 55). Humans "wear [a] frail body" and therefore "cannot be without sin" (1.22; 56; cf. 4.51). Though Thomas' view of the body might appear extreme, it is important to keep in mind that he, like many spiritual authors before him, think of the body as the initial way that sin secures a foothold.[27] Our natural need to eat, albeit in moderation, becomes immoderate and leads to gluttony whereas our natural desire to procreate leads fallen humankind to lust. By following our "natural inclinations" (*sensualitatem*) alone we "defile" our "conscience, and lose the grace of God" (1.1; 28).[28] Similar to Augustine of Hippo, Thomas concludes that "we have lost our innocence through sin" (1.22; 56).[29]

A proper response to humankind's fallen and sinful state, it seems, is to meditate on one's impending death.[30] Because death is "at hand" it behooves the devout person to "consider . . . the state of [her] soul." In typical *ars moriendi*-style, Thomas advises, "You should order your every deed and thought, as though today were the day of your death"

27. See, for example, John Cassian, *Conferences* 5.3.
28. On Thomas' theology of grace, see chapter 5 below.
29. See Augustine of Hippo, *Confessions* 1.7.11.
30. Book 1.22 ("On Human Misery") is followed immediately by "A Meditation on Death." It would seem that programmatically these chapters go together inasmuch as spiritual and physical death is the ultimate consequence of human sin.

(1.23; 57).³¹ In Thomas' estimation, there is no use for a long life if one does not, each day, strive to amend one's life, for "Blessed is the man who keeps the hour of his death always in mind, and daily prepares himself to die.... Each morning remember that you may not live until evening; and in the evening, do not presume to promise yourself another day" (1.23; 58). Death is every human being's natural end, therefore, there is no escape but only dutiful and proper preparation. Thomas writes that a happy death will be found in "perfect contempt of the world; fervent desire to grow in holiness; love of discipline; the practice of penance; ready obedience; self-denial; [and] the bearing of every trial for the love of Christ" (1.23; 58).

Perfect Contempt of the World

By the fifteenth century the idea of "contempt of the world" (*contemptus mundi*) was well established and a common Christian theme. For example, Bernard of Cluny, sometime between the 1120s to 1150s, wrote his *De contemptu mundi*, a "Bitter Satirical Poem of 3000 Lines upon the Morals of the XIIth Century."³² Though, in the words of one reviewer, the work "is not much more than a tissue of commonplaces,"³³ its contents are meant to shake the reader back into a concern for heavenly things and a scorn for the things of the world. "The hour of doom is at hand; the times are out of joint. Let us awake!," writes Bernard.³⁴ "Run, good man," he continues, "avoid the slipper, and choose the virtuous."³⁵

---

31. On the "Art of Dying" (*ars moriendi*) tradition in the late Middle Ages, see Forcén and Forcén, "*Ars Moriendi*."

32. This is the subtitle of Hoskier, ed., *De contemptu mundi*.

33. Mann, "Review of Ronald E. Pepin, *Scorn for the World*," 163.

34. Preble and Jackson, "The Scorn of the World," 78.

35. Preble and Jackson, "The Scorn of the World," 80.

Thomas' Spiritual Theology I

Thomas would completely agree! He begins the *Imitation* by admonishing his readers not to seek honors and not "to be a slave to bodily desires" (*carnis desideria*). Further, "It is vanity to wish for a long life. . . . It is vanity to give thought only to the present life. . . . It is vanity to love things that so swiftly pass away." Rather, the devout person will "despise the world [*contemptum mundi*], and draw daily nearer to the kingdom of heaven" (1.1; 28).

Contempt of this world is also manifested in a desire for the next world: "O ever-blessed palaces of the heavenly City! O glorious day of eternity! . . . O day of unending gladness! . . . How greatly I long for the dawning of this day, and the end of all worldly things," writes the "disciple" (4.48; 156). That which is heavenly is longed for fervently because in life the devout person is defiled by sin, ensnared by passions, prey to fears, entangled in vanities, hedged in by errors, worn out by labors, burdened by temptations, exhausted by pleasures, and tormented by want. The true disciple of God longs to be in God's presence, alongside the other saints of God, so that her evils will come to an end, she will be set free from her slavery to sin, her mind will be fixed on God alone, she will experience fullness of joy, and will "enjoy true freedom, untrammelled [*sic*] and untroubled in mind or body." In short, "Everything that this world offers me as comfort is utterly distasteful; I long for close communion with You" (4.48; 157).

For Thomas, this desire for heavenly things and strong rejection of that which is worldly comes from God himself. This "desire for eternal blessedness" is of "heavenly origin" (4.49; 159). Nonetheless, there is a very strong disdain, or even hatred, for the body in Thomas' thought that would seem hard to think of as God-given. In fact, he goes so far as to refer to the body as a "prison" from which the devout person needs to escape (*de tabernaculo corporis exire concupiscis*) because the body holds one back from contemplating God's "unchanging glory" (4.49; 159).[36] Such a negative view of the body creates the rhetorical space for Thomas to highlight the spiritually salvific role of God's gracious intervention, but it seems surprisingly dismissive of the fact that the human body is also the good work of God's creation (see Gen 1:26–27). It also seems to undermine Thomas' robust Eucharistic theology wherein he writes that the "spiritual grace" of the sacrament restores the soul *and* the body: "Such is the grace of this Sacrament, that from the fullness of devotion You afford greater powers not only to the mind, but to the frail body" (3.1; 186–187). The body is not to be hated, but it does need to be kept under godly control by way of self-denial.

Self-Denial

The practice of self-denial falls under the general rubric of asceticism. In the early church, ἄσκησις/*askēsis* referred to the study of the sacred scriptures,[37] bodily discipline,[38] and served as a technical term for the monastic life.[39] Jordan Aumann writes that "a Polish Franciscan named Dobrosielski introduced the word *ascetical* into the Latin usage of western theology in 1655"[40] and thereafter, especially among Roman Catholic writers of the early nineteenth century, a distinction was made between ascetical theology and other areas of theology. For example, according to Adolphe Tanquerey, ascetical theology is one of the three

36. On the body as a prison see also 3.11; 205: "the prison-house of this body" (*carcere corporis*).
37. Origen of Alexandria, *Contra Celsus* 7.60.
38. Basil of Caesarea, *Ep.* 81.1.
39. Athanasius of Alexandria, *Life of Anthony*, Prologue.
40. Aumann, *Spiritual Theology*, 14.

parts of theology, the others being dogmatic and moral. For Tanquerey, ascetical theology has its foundation in dogma that depends upon and completes moral theology—ascetical theology directs dogmatic truths toward practice and moves beyond moral theology in that it insists "on a higher degree of virtue than strictly obligatory. Ascetical Theology, then, is truly *the science of Christian perfection*."[41] But apart from the formal discipline of "ascetical theology," ἄσκησις/*askēsis* literally means exercise, practice, or training. Thus, self-denial is for the purpose of training oneself for godliness (see 1 Tim 4:7–8). In Thomas' estimation, a devout person "who is not yet perfectly dead to self is easily tempted, and is overcome even in small and trifling things" (1.6; 33–34).

In Thomas' thought, the saints are held up as examples of those who practiced appropriate self-denial: "they strove with all their might to mortify in themselves all worldly desires, and could thus cling to God in their inmost heart, and offer themselves freely and wholly to Him" (1.11; 37). The monastic desert fathers set the same example, says Thomas: "How strict and self-denying was the life of the holy Fathers in the desert! . . . How strict their fasts! . . . They renounced all riches, dignities, honours, friends and kindred" (1.18; 46–47). Acts of bodily mortification or self-denial include, for example, avoiding unnecessary talking (1.10 and 20), practicing solitude (1.20), disciplining the senses (1.21), resisting our bodily appetites (i.e., "taking no account of what the body likes or dislikes, and [struggling] to subdue the unwilling flesh to the spirit"; 4.11; 108), and fasting. Unsurprisingly Jesus and his cross are the great exemplars of self-denial for only Jesus is free from all self-interest and self-love: "how powerful is the pure love of Jesus, free from all self-interest and self-love" (2.2; 83). In a moving passage

---

41. Tanquerey, *The Spiritual Life*, 5; italics in the original.

Thomas contrasts the actions of Jesus over against the actions of his followers. Jesus desired suffering, but his followers desire comfort. Many are willing to feast with Jesus, but few are willing to fast. All rejoice with Jesus, but few are willing to suffer. His miracles are admired, but his humiliation on the cross is ignored. Lastly, "Many follow Jesus to the Breaking of Bread, but few to the drinking of the Cup of His Passion" (2.2; 83).

Self-denial is not just bodily mortification, though that is often how it has been understood in the tradition.[42] It is also a mortification of the desires or other vices and sins that are less corporeal. The foundation of rightly ordered desire is found in the Lord's Prayer: God's "will be done" (Matt 6:10). Our desiring faculty is from God but it is corrupted by sin.[43] If our desire was not corrupted it would desire and will in line with God's will. But it does not desire and will well in its sinful state. Thus, our desires are often tainted by our willingness, even eagerness, to sin. Moreover, our unwillingness to will rightly is rooted in self-love, wherein we put our own desires before our desire for God (4.13). Thomas recognizes that not every desire comes from God by way of the Holy Spirit, even if it is a good and right desire. Because of this we need to deny ourselves our desires unless moved by God to use them to his glory (4.15; 112). Further, the grace of God is needed in order for the believer to will in a way that is pleasing and acceptable to God (see 4.53).

42. See Finn, *Asceticism in the Graeco-Roman World*, 58–155.

43. The goodness of the human desiring faculty is seen in Eve's understanding (and presumably in Adam's too) that the tree of the knowledge of good and evil in the Garden of Eden "was to be desired to make one wise" (Gen 3:16). It is true that the tree would in fact make one wise since it was a tree "of knowledge." Eve and Adam's sin was not in desiring *per se* but in eating from the tree after God had forbidden them from doing so.

Thomas' Spiritual Theology I

In Book 4, chapters 32–33, Thomas offers his most sustained treatment of the renunciation of desires. First, because humans are obsessed with self-interest and self-love, they are slaves to their desires. But if they renounce desire then they will be at peace and if they set their heart on "higher things" then, in time, they will "stand ready to do [God's] will" (4.32; 137). Thus, the renunciation of our desires is a heart issue; that is, an interior disposition that must be cultivated. Thomas is committed to a fundamental principle, which he may have learned from John Cassian: "When our inner inclinations [*interior affectus*] are corrupted, the actions that spring from them are also corrupted. And this is a sign of our lack of inner strength; and from a pure heart alone springs the fruit of a holy life" (4.31; 136).[44] A devout person must attend to her heart if she hopes to renounce desire (see 4.27; 131: "A Prayer for a Pure Heart and Heavenly Wisdom"). Thus, her heart must be constant and singularly focused. Thomas warns the believer not to trust her affections because "they are changeable and inconstant." But a spiritually mature person "stands above these changing emotions" and "remain[s] single in purpose" (*simplici intentionis oculo*). In fact, the "more single his purpose" (*purior fuerit intentionis oculus*) the more steady and constant he becomes. "Therefore," Thomas concludes, "make your intention pure, single [*simplex*], and upright, that it may be directed to [God] alone without hindrance" (4.33; 138–39). And, "To live inwardly to God . . . is the proper state of a spiritual man" (2.6; 75).

Ready Obedience

As mentioned before, one of the issues that lies at the root of an inability to renounce desire is self-love. Though the

44. See Stewart, *Cassian the Monk*, 41–48.

Scriptures command love of God and love of neighbor (Matt 22:37–39), self-love makes this difficult for "Seldom is anyone so spiritual as to strip himself entirely of self-love" (2.2; 83). Moreover, love of self hinders the devout person's ability to stand in obedience to God and his commandments and ultimately leads to a multitude of other sins, including pride. So, self-love must be dealt with if one expects to progress spiritually: "If you aspire to reach this height of perfection, you must make a brave beginning. Lay the axe to the roots, to cut out and destroy all inordinate and secret love of self, and of any personal and material advantage. From this vice of inordinate self-love spring nearly all those other failings that have to be completely overcome" (4.53; 168).[45]

Thomas' words against self-love get at the root of humankind's sin-sickness for self-love hurts the devout person more than anything else in the world (4.27). Thomas acknowledges that everything imprisons the heart to some degree, and that imprisonment is in direct proportion to the degree of love that one has for that thing. In an Augustinian sense, distorted love is not a distinct kind of love, for there is only a true "kind" of love, so much as the love of something in a twisted way.[46] For example, it is good to love a friend, but not for himself or for his sake but for God's sake. Love, for Augustine, is synonymous with the Holy Spirit, who is the divine love that both is God and from God. Love moves believers to appreciate and desire God above everything else and to love self, neighbor, and all lower goods for the sake of God's goodness: "every human being, *qua* human being, should be loved on God's account; and God should be loved for himself."[47] Thus, there can be

---

45. A properly ordered self-love will be discussed below.
46. See Augustine of Hippo, *Sermon* 330.2.
47. Augustine of Hippo, *On Christian Teaching* 1.28.28; Green,

Thomas' Spiritual Theology I

a kind of proper self-love, but only if that self-love moves beyond the self to God. As Oliver O'Donovan rightly notes, "the idea of self-love in St. Augustine of Hippo constitutes a problem. Self-love is loving God; it is also hating God."[48] Love of self that results in love of God is a rightly ordered love but self-love that ends at the self demonstrates hatred towards God.[49] Thomas is concerned with the latter.

It appears, for Thomas, that self-love manifests itself through our desire to want to possess things and to subject ourselves to them to such an extent that we become their slave (4.27). This care about things shows that we are not putting our trust in God and, by extension, shows our lack of love for God. Though Thomas does not reach this conclusion explicitly, such a perspective suggests that poverty (of both material things and also "of spirit," as in Matt 5:3) would be rooted in a correct love of God. Poverty is evidence of trust in God wholeheartedly as is love of God. That is, someone who loves God well does not "exhaust" herself with grief or "burden" herself with "needless anxieties." Rather, she trusts God's goodwill towards her, freeing herself from the things that keep her from loving God: "Our advantage does not consist in winning or increasing possessions; it lies rather in being indifferent to such things, and eradicating the desire for them from our hearts" (4.27; 130). This inordinate need for other things draws us away from God and they become the focus of our love (which is actually an expression of our self-love) because we wrongly assume that we cannot live without them. Without love for God obedience to him is out of the question. Thus, the devout person must "conquer self," especially one's self-love, "to advance in holiness" (1.3; 31).

---

trans., *Saint Augustine: On Christian Teaching*, 21.

48. O'Donovan, *The Problem of Self-Love in St. Augustine*, 1.

49. See also chapter 6 below.

Fervent Desire to Grow in Holiness

One of the great ironies of the Christian spiritual tradition is that overcoming self-love actually requires self-knowledge—we move beyond ourselves by attention to the self.[50] Thomas appears to be working within a Cistercian framework in this regard. In his *On Loving God*, Bernard of Clairvaux wrote that there are four degrees of love: 1) a person loves himself for his own sake; 2) a person loves God for one's own advantage; 3) a person loves God for God's sake; and 4) a person loves himself for the sake of God.[51] All love has God as its source for he "is the efficient and final cause of our love. He offers the opportunity, creates the affection, and consummates the desire."[52] Moreover, "Love is not imposed by a precept; it is planted in nature,"[53] making it possible for all persons to know themselves and, in this way, come to love themselves, albeit selfishly. Nonetheless, it is this initial self-love that sets one on course to come, with God's grace, to a knowledge of God: "In this way, man [*sic*] who is animal and carnal, and knows how to love only himself, yet starts loving God for his own benefit, because he learns from frequent experience that he can do everything that is good for him in God and that without God he can do nothing good."[54] Not everyone comes to the fourth

50. See, for example, Osborne, Jr., *Love of Self and Love of God*.

51. Bernard's influence on Thomas is particularly evident when he writes, "They who love Jesus for His own sake, and not for the sake of comfort for themselves" (2.2; 83); and, "Let me love You more than myself, and myself only for Your own sake" (4.5; 98–99).

52. Bernard of Clairvaux, *On Loving God* VIII.22; Conway and Walton, trans. *Bernard of Clairvaux*, 114.

53. Bernard of Clairvaux, *On Loving God* VIII.23; Conway and Walton, trans. *Bernard of Clairvaux*, 115.

54. Bernard of Clairvaux, *On Loving God* VIII.25; Conway and Walton, trans. *Bernard of Clairvaux*, 117.

degree of love but everyone has the same opportunity to begin the journey by way of self-knowledge and self-love. Thus, the most necessary kind of knowledge for the person being spiritually formed is self-knowledge: "There are two facts you should know: first, what you are; secondly, that you are not that by your own power, lest you fail to boast at all or do so in vain. . . . [K]now yourself."[55]

Knowledge itself is a gift of God, concludes Thomas, especially when that knowledge comes from "Truth itself" and not just from "signs and passing words."[56] But knowledge for knowledge's sake alone often just leads to controversy and makes the devout person "deliberately turn to curious and harmful things," which is "supreme folly" (1.3; 30). In the end, "true learning is good in itself and ordained by God; but a good conscience and a holy life are always to be preferred." Further, a "humble knowledge of oneself is a surer road to God than a deep searching of the sciences" (1.3; 31). Knowledge of the mysteries of God is always preferable to knowledge of the sciences (4.43). For Thomas, there is a direct correlation between what you know and the severity of God's judgment, for knowledge is primarily for the sake of one's growth in holiness (1.2). Thus, the holy Christian will "Restrain an inordinate desire for knowledge" (1.2; 28) and will mostly turn her rational faculty towards knowing herself, for it is in self-knowledge that one can begin the journey to union with God.

By coming to know oneself, the devout Christian is able to address her inordinate desires and understand rightly the laws and commandments of God. True knowledge

---

55. Bernard of Clairvaux, *On Loving God* II.4; Conway and Walton, trans., *Bernard of Clairvaux*, 96.

56. See Augustine of Hippo's *On the Teacher* in which Augustine asserts that it is God, as the inner Teacher, who helps us come to the truth though we do make use of words as signs.

is purifying for it brings to light those things that need eradication through self-denial for what the mind, through knowledge, "conceives as desirable is always to be desired and sought only in the fear of God and with a humble heart" (4.15; 113). Reciprocally, the more one grows in holiness the more he is able to understand (1.3; cf. 1.4). As well, God has not left the devout person on her own, says Thomas, but provides wise counsel through others in order to bring forth greater godly knowledge: "Take counsel of a wise and conscientious man, and seek to be guided by one who is better than yourself, rather than follow your own opinions" (1.4; 32); and "ask counsel of one who is wise and fears God" (1.8; 35). Such submission to a spiritual elder rests on the virtues of obedience (1.9) and silence,[57] for talkativeness is a vice, writes Thomas. The one who desires to grow in holiness only speaks to edify others and it is only "devout conversation on spiritual matters" that "greatly furthers . . . spiritual progress" (1.10; 27). And it is only in silence and quietness that the devout soul "learns the hidden mysteries of the Scriptures" (1.20; 51). But the Scriptures must not be read "to satisfy curiosity or to pass the time" but, instead, to move one's "heart to devotion" (1.20; 50).[58]

Importantly for Thomas, this silence and quietude invokes a love of solitude since it creates the space necessary

---

57. Thomas' teaching to "live under obedience to a superior" (1.9; 36) is likely inspired by the sixth-century *Rule of Benedict*. Benedict's influence is seen elsewhere in the *Imitation*. For example, "We must revere Him above all things" (1.19; 48) echoes the *Rule of Benedict* 5.2: "cherish Christ above all" (Fry, ed., *RB 1980*, 187); and, "account yourself the least of all men" (2.2; 70) echoes the *Rule of Benedict* 7.51: "The seventh step of humility is that a man not only admits with his tongue but is also convinced in his heart that he is inferior to all and of less value" (Fry, ed., *RB 1980*, 198).

58. On the medieval conception of curiosity (*curiositas*) as a vice see Thomas Aquinas, *Summa Theologiae* 2a2ae, q. 167, arts. 1–2.

for "meditation on holy things" (1.20; 50). Such solitude is not only in imitation of the great saints (1.18) but is also in imitation of Jesus who withdrew from crowds (e.g., Luke 5:16). The devout Christian must withdraw into her own inner cell. Though a monastic, Thomas did not limit the concept of "cell" to the monk's physical cell in the monastery.[59] Rather, and perhaps more importantly, everyone has an inner cell so that every believer can withdraw into solitude at any time, and even find delight in dwelling there. This makes it possible to avoid preoccupation with "worldly affairs," creating the space for peace and tranquility that leads to thinking "only on divine and salutary things" (1.20; 51). Keeping one's mind in the world leads to a disquieted heart (1.20; 53) but he who withdraws has God draw near to him. In drawing near to us God regulates our hearts to overcome our sinful inclinations and orients us toward cultivating the virtues by way of spiritual exercises and discipline.

Love of Discipline

Though he is speaking about vowed religious like himself, Thomas' comments on the good practices of those living the monastic life are applicable to all the devout. This is all the more so given his spiritualizing of the monastic cell, as discussed above. Besides, Thomas would agree wholeheartedly with Jordan of Quedlinburg's sentiment, referenced in

59. The fourteenth-century text *The Abbey of the Holy Ghost*, for example, also talks about the monastic life as something that is interior to each believer: "My dear brothers and sisters, I can well see that many wish to enter religion, but may not do so on account of poverty, or out of dread, or for fear of their relatives, or because of the tie of marriage. Therefore I here draw up a book of religion of the heart, that is, of the Abbey of the Holy Ghost, so that all those who may not physically enter religion may do so spiritually" (Swanson, trans., *Catholic England*, 96).

chapter 3 above, that "the habit does not make the monk":[60] the "habit and tonsure of themselves are of small significance; it is the transformation of one's way of life and the complete mortification of the passions that make a true Religious" (1.17; 45). Accordingly, the "life of a good Religious should shine with all the virtues, that he may be inwardly as he appears outwardly to men. Indeed, there should be far more inward goodness than appears outwardly, for God Himself searches all hearts" (1.19; 48).[61] Though it is what is on the inside that is of greatest importance (see Matt 15:18–20), this does not mean that the outward can be neglected. For Thomas, as for much of the Christian spiritual tradition, there is a symbiosis between the outer and inner in a person and "both are vital to our advance" (1.19; 48). If one neglects her spiritual exercises then she experiences loss in her soul, unless she omits them in order to perform an act of mercy or help another believer (1.19; 48).[62] And if her soul, due to sloth, for example, fails to engender proper fervor, then her spiritual exercises are omitted. And when spiritual exercises, which differ from one believer to another (1.19; 49), are omitted or lightened unnecessarily there is a breakdown in the devout person's discipline.

Discipline, for Thomas, is what characterizes the devout/monastic life (1.17; cf. 1.25). A person who is truly zealous for holiness accepts and obeys all commands and is content to follow the rule because to do otherwise would be to expose himself to "dreadful ruin" (1.25; 65). Thomas holds up the Carthusians, the Cistercians, and other monks and nuns as examples of well-disciplined religious whose

60. Saak, *High Way to Heaven*, 219, fn. 216.

61. This dichotomy between inward and outward, especially in a monastic context, may have come from John Cassian. See Peters, *The Monkhood of All Believers*, 33.

62. On the concept of "spiritual exercises" see chapter 2 above.

example should be followed. These monks and nuns "guard themselves with discipline" so that they progress in holiness. Thomas even goes so far as to say that the more disciplined one is, the greater will be one's spiritual progress. Discipline leads to the acquisition of virtue and godliness (1.25). A true disciple and devout person will ask God to instruct her in discipline (4.5), knowing that to live under God's holy discipline brings "heavenly sweetness" (4.20; 120)[63] and needful correction (4.50). The disciplined disciple, progressing in virtue and holiness, is then able to move beyond purgation, into illumination.

ILLUMINATION

The illuminative state is, in particular, associated with the cultivation of virtue. Having taken stock of sinful human nature and prescribed the proper remedies in the purgative stage, the devout person is now able to focus on becoming virtuous, in particular through the cultivation of humility and in practicing other virtues. In Thomas' thought, the devout person "should shine with all the virtues" (1.19; 48 cf. 1.20) and she who is most virtuous demonstrates that she has matured beyond those still in purgation (see 1.25). In short, the "true lover of Christ" is an "eager seeker after" virtue (2.9; 79).[64] In particular, Thomas focuses on the virtues of humility, patience, and prudence/wisdom.

63. Though Sherley-Price translates Thomas to say "to live under God's holy rule," the Latin is *sancta disciplina*, which is more accurately translated "holy discipline."

64. Sherley-Price translates *virtutum* as "holiness," but more properly it means "virtue."

Humility

In the medieval church, pride was the greatest vice and the root of all other sins. Thomas Aquinas, for example, thinks that pride is the most grievous of sins.[65] That being the case, humility then becomes the greatest virtue, exemplified by Jesus Christ himself in the incarnation:

> Have this mind among yourselves, which is yours in Christ Jesus, who, though he was in the form of God, did not count equality with God a thing to be grasped, but made himself nothing, taking the form of a servant, being born in the likeness of men. And being found in human form, he humbled himself by becoming obedient to the point of death, even death on a cross. Therefore God has highly exalted him and bestowed on him the name that is above every name. (Phil. 2:5–9)

Thomas first situates humility as a positive result of knowing one's faults: "It is often good for us that others know and expose our faults, for so may we be kept humble." Instead of relying on oneself, the devout person will submit herself to God and make light of those who may speak against her (cf. 4.28). She will welcome this because in knowing her faults she knows whom she has offended and can be reconciled to them. Such transparency and vulnerability are the result of humility, and it is the humble whom

---

65. *Summa Theologiae* 2a2ae, q. 162, art. 6. The sin of avarice was sometimes also viewed as the greatest sin. See Little, *Religious Poverty and the Profit Economy in Medieval Europe*, 36: "Until the end of the tenth century, pride was unreservedly dominant as the most important vice; writers who dealt with avarice tended to reduce it to a sub-category of pride. But in the eleventh century, Peter Damian heralded a significant change when stating unequivocally: 'Avarice is the root of all evil.'" See also Newhauser, *The Early History of Greed*.

God loves and protects. It is the humble that God exalts, in imitation of Christ. It is to the humble that God "reveals his secrets, and lovingly calls and draws him to Himself" (2.2; 70). Humility in light of one's faults allows the believer to know the truth and to be set free by the truth because he will no longer be living self-deceived about his own spiritual progress. Truth with humility reminds the devout person that he must not boast but rather be ashamed, remembering his sinfulness and that he is weighed down by his passions. In the end, truly humble disciples "always tend to nothing" (4.4; 96: *semper ad nihil tendis*; cf. 4.40).[66]

Thomas acknowledges that the devout person may be tempted to boast about her devotion; that is, that she has received the "grace of devotion." Therefore, Thomas advises her to think more humbly of herself, recognizing instead that this grace has been given to one desperately in need of it. In other words, she has been given this grace *because* she is unworthy and without it she would be sad and needy. She has not merited it through any goodness or worthiness of her own but only through God's goodness. Somewhat ironically, Thomas believes that one's spiritual progress "consists not so much in enjoying the grace of consolation, as in bearing its withdrawal with humility, resignation and patience" (4.7; 101). Moreover, a devout person's "merit" is on display, in part, when he is "grounded in humility [*humilitate*] . . . by his low esteem [*nihil reputet*] and honest depreciation [*veritate despiciat*] of himself; and by his preference for humiliation [*humiliari*] and despite [*despici*] rather than honours at the hands of men [*sic*]" (4.7; 103). The disciple recognizes that she is but dust and ashes so she humbles herself and acknowledges her nothingness before God (4.8; cf. 4.13; 110: "you, who are dust and

---

66. On this concept of the human person tending towards nothingness see Athanasius of Alexandria, *On the Incarnation* 4.5 and 6.4.

nothingness"). The depth of this humiliation is captured well when Thomas writes that "the last trace of self-esteem be engulfed in the depth of my nothingness . . . for I am nothing. . . . By myself I am nothing" (4.8; 104). Such radical self-loathing ("perverse self-love," in Thomas' language) is *not* rooted in a twisted psychosis but in a conviction that one sees oneself most clearly when one knows God most properly. In yet another moment of dependence on Augustine of Hippo, Thomas says, "by lovingly seeking You alone, I have found both myself and You" (4.8; 104).[67] In human debasement God is lifted up and exalted and human nature is viewed properly: "How humble and insignificant I am! . . . I acknowledge my utter nothingness! . . . I recognize myself as wholly and only nothing!" (4.14; 112).

In her nothingness and from her humility, the devout believer understands that her only hope in life and death is to call upon God, asking him to make her into something from nothing (*creatio ex nihilo*). From this same place of humility and nothingness, however, she is also able to shun worldly honors and advancement (4.41). Deceived by vanity the disciple seeks affirmation from the people and things of the earth, finding in them only a false peace for true peace comes from God alone. But Thomas goes further by reminding the disciple that even one's friends and family must be despised if one wants to truly imitate Christ for "If anyone comes after [Christ] and does not hate his own father and mother and wife and children and brothers and sisters, yes, and even his own life, he cannot be [Christ's] disciple" (Luke 14:26). The devout person mortifies his familial affection and forgoes human companionship because there is a direct correlation between affection for others and

---

67. See Augustine of Hippo, *Confessions* 10.1.1: "May I know you, who know me. May I 'know as I also am known'" (Chadwick, trans., *Saint Augustine: Confessions*, 178).

affection for God: the disciple "draws nearer to God as he withdraws further from the consolations of this world. And the deeper he descends into himself and the lower he regards himself, the higher he ascends towards God" (4.42; 148).[68]

Patience

The virtue of patience bears two connotations: peace and endurance. Thomas says that a peaceful person brings peace to others and that it is more beneficial to be peaceful than learned. The peaceful believer thinks well of people, which allows him to look after his own affairs because he is not attempting to notice what is wrong in others. Further, a peaceful person is no trouble to others. True peace, says Thomas, depends "on humble forbearance rather than on the absence of adversity." It is born out of the "secret of endurance" (2.3; 71). And endurance comes when a disciple carries her cross as opposed to seeking pleasure. This rejection of comfort produces patience (2.10). Alas, however, there are "many who desire comfort, but few who desire suffering" (2.11; 83) despite the truth that it is only suffering that produces endurance (i.e., patience; Rom 5:3). "And," writes Thomas, "if you share His sufferings, you will also share His glory" (2.12; 85). So every devout person should follow the "royal road of the Holy Cross" (2.12; 86), resolving to bear the cross in order to prepare "to endure many trials and obstacles in this vale of tears" (2.12; 87). Patience is born through endurance.

At the same time, however, patience is also born in the quotidian trials of life, including the lack that comes by way

---

68. See Augustine of Hippo, *Confessions* 4.12.19: "Come down so that you can ascend, and make your ascent to God" (Chadwick, trans., *Saint Augustine: Confessions*, 64).

of proper self-denial and contempt of the world. Though the rich have all that they want and need, their riches will "vanish like smoke" and even in this life they do not enjoy them "without bitterness, weariness and fear." The rich live in fear of losing what they have, whereas those who have given up these things receive godly consolation: "in the despising of worldly things and in the shunning of base delights shall be your blessing, and you shall win abundant consolation. The more you withdraw yourself from the comfort of creatures, the sweeter and more potent will be the consolations that you will find in Me" (4.12; 109). In the end, the devout person needs to remind herself that her trials and sufferings are small in comparison to those endured by Christ and the martyrs, for example (see 4.47). Elevating one's minor sufferings too much is not only a sign of impatience but a spurning of the "merit of patience" (4.19; 117). A truly patient person accepts these things gladly because he knows that they ultimately come "as from the hand of God" (4.19; 118; cf. 4.29) who does not test believers beyond their level of endurance (cf. 1 Cor. 10:13).

Prudence

Prudence, for Christian theologians of the early and medieval church, is the virtue that makes it possible for the believer to know what to seek after and what to avoid.[69] It is a kind of wisdom. Thomas regularly notes that devout persons turn away from what is good to pursue things that are harmful (e.g., 1.3). But some people also pursue seemingly good things inordinately. As noted above, Thomas thought that study and knowledge were good, but he also warns that even this good thing can go too far because,

69. See, for example, Thomas Aquinas, *Summa Theologiae* 2a2ae, q. 47, arts. 1, who quotes Augustine of Hippo.

Thomas' Spiritual Theology I

in the end, it is not what one knows that matters but how one lives (1.3; 31).[70] Too much study, coupled with wrong ends (e.g., worldly knowledge) will likely lead to the sin of curiosity (1.5). The prudent person, however, will count "earthly things as dung" in order live a properly balanced life to "win Christ" (1.3; 32).[71] Furthermore, a prudent person will test the wisdom of other's words and his own internal feelings and seek guidance from someone who is more advanced in holiness (1.4). Yet, even these prudent counselors will, in the end, prove limited in their helpfulness (4.59). All earthly sources of wisdom come up short. Only God, the infinitely wise one (3.3), can, in the end, be the surest guide: "It is a great art to know how to hold converse with Jesus, and to know how to keep Jesus is wisdom [*prudentia*] indeed" (2.8; 77). And: "Teach me, O Lord, to do Your will; teach me to live worthily and humbly in Your sight; for You are my Wisdom" (4.3; 95).

Thomas makes a distinction between worldly wisdom and heavenly wisdom (see, in particular, 4.32) with the latter, of course, being the more valuable of the two. Thomas sums the distinction up well when he writes, "There is a great difference between the wisdom of a devout man [*sic*] enlightened by God, and the knowledge of a learned and studious scholar. More noble by far is the learning infused from above . . . than that painfully acquired by the industry of man [*sic*]" (4.31; 136). The so-called "worldly-wise" (4.34; 139) actually lack God's wisdom, making their wisdom a kind of pseudo-wisdom, if you will. Perhaps their "wisdom" is right and correct (e.g., that 2+2=4), but it lacks the

---

70. For a commendation of study see, for example, 4.11; 155: "Write, study, worship, be penitent, keep silence, and pray."

71. Though Sherley-Price translates *prudens* as "wise" in 1.3, it can be rendered more literally as "prudent."

seasoning of God's wisdom that yields sweet savor (4.34).[72] All devout believers must seek after heavenly wisdom since it is the only true wisdom and leads to God: "Grant me heavenly wisdom, O Lord, that above all else I may learn to search for and discover You; to know and love You; and to see all things as they really are, and as You in Your wisdom have ordered them" (4.27; 131). As devout persons long for this heavenly wisdom and gratefully receive it, they must also long for he who is Wisdom, earnestly seeking and working to be unioned with him.

PERFECTION; OR, UNION WITH GOD

Throughout Christian history the church's theologians have said that not everyone, at least in this life, will be graced by God with a personal experience of the divine presence. Full blessedness awaits the devout follower of Jesus in heaven, at the final consummation of all time when every faithful disciple will see God face to face and know him fully (cf. 1 Cor 13:12). Such an experience cannot be merited through human action but always comes by the grace of God: a "soul needs much grace to be raised up and carried [*rapiat*] beyond itself" (4.31; 135). Bernard of Clairvaux, for example, writes, "It is in a spiritual and immortal body, calm and pleasant, subject to the spirit in everything, that the soul hopes to attain the fourth degree of love [i.e., union with God], or rather to be possessed by it; for it is in God's hands to give it to whom he wishes, it is not obtained by human efforts."[73] Bernard also says that union with God is

---

72. Sherley-Price seems to have omitted an entire phrase from his translation of 4.34: *sed si debet gratum esse et bene sapere, oportet gratiam tuam adesse, et condimento tuæ sapientiæ condiri* ("but if it would be pleasant and of sweet savor, your grace must be there, and it is your wisdom which must give it a sweet savor").

73. Bernard of Clairvaux, *On Loving God* X.29; Conway and Walton, trans. *Bernard of Clairvaux*, 121.

infrequent and transitory: "If any mortal, suddenly rapt... and for a moment is admitted to this... brotherly love calls him back. Alas, he has to come back to himself, to descend again into his being."[74] Thomas would agree.

"Above all things and in all things rest always in the Lord, O my soul, for He is the everlasting rest of the Saints," writes Thomas (4.21; 120). Proper Christian rest, then, is only found in God and it is the devout person's *telos*, her final end: "I must be your supreme and final End" (4.9; 104: *ego debeo esse finis tuus supremus*). On earth this rest might look like *apatheia* (freedom from sinful passions) but eschatologically it is much more than that, perhaps best depicted in the Middle Ages by Dante Alighieri's *Paradisio*, though Thomas was likely influenced more by Augustine of Hippo's dramatic vision of God at Ostia.[75] For Thomas the person most at rest is the woman of singular purpose, or single-eyed (4.31: *simplici oculo*). This devout person's singular focus, trained on God, can yield a moment of union with God in which she is "Rapt in spirit" so as to "rise above all created things" in order to "see clearly" (*se ipsum perfecte deserere ac in excessu mentis stare, et videre te omnium Conditorem cum creaturis nil simile habere*). What constitutes this union with God is that believers leave behind created things, including themselves, in order to "free themselves entirely from transitory things" (4.31; 135: *sciunt se a perituris creaturis ad plenum sequestrari*).[76]

---

74. Bernard of Clairvaux, *On Loving God* X.27; Conway and Walton, trans. *Bernard of Clairvaux*, 119–20.

75. See Augustine of Hippo, *Confessions* 9.10.

76. This is further evidence of Thomas dependence on Augustine of Hippo, who writes, "The conversation led us [i.e., Augustine and his mother Monica] towards the conclusion that the pleasure of the bodily senses, however delightful in the radiant light of this physical world, is seen by comparison with the life of eternity to be not even worth considering. Our minds were lifted up by an ardent affection

As he is raised up to God, set free from earthly things, the believer is "wholly united to God" (4.31; 136: *Deo totus unitus*). But like Bernard, Thomas thinks that this rapture out of oneself (*in excessum subito raperis*) is transitory and one will "swiftly return to the usual trivial thoughts" (4.6; 100). Nonetheless, this ecstasy with God should be sought by all devout persons and every true disciple must know that his ascetic efforts and cultivation of virtue culminate, by God's will, in union with God, in full eschatologically, but perhaps in passing even now.

DISCUSSION QUESTIONS

1. Why is interiority fundamental to the work of *Imitation of Christ*?
2. What is the relationship between purging and pleasure?
3. What are the various *skopos* of the three stages of ascension, and how do they tie to the overall *telos* of ascension?
4. Does moving towards God mean moving toward or away from the self?
5. How is humility essential to ascension?

---

towards eternal being itself. Step by step we climbed beyond all corporeal objects and the heaven itself, where sun, moon, and stars shed light on the earth. We ascended even further by internal reflection and dialogue and wonder at your works, and we entered into our own minds" (*Confessions* 9.10.24; Chadwick, trans., *Saint Augustine: Confessions*, 171).

5

THOMAS' SPIRITUAL THEOLOGY II

The Imitation of Christ

INTRODUCTION

THIS CHAPTER WILL CONSIDER two themes that are related and are important in Thomas' *Imitation*: grace and the blessed sacrament. A superficial reading of the *Imitation* may lead the reader to think that Thomas does not care much about grace; that is, that his spiritual theology is too heavily dependent on the will and efforts of the devout person and not sufficiently undergirded by a robust theology of grace.[1] Given Thomas' indebtedness to Augustine of Hippo, such a view would be odd.[2] As it turns out, Thomas speaks

---

1. For example, Thomas admonishes his readers, "Endeavour, then, to make progress . . . Labour for a short while now" (1.25; 63), but does not explicitly connect this endeavoring and laboring to grace.

2. Perhaps the most explicit evidence of Thomas' familiarity with

101

frequently about grace. As mentioned in chapter 4 above, the original manuscript ordering of the books of the *Imitation* placed "On the [Blessed] Sacrament" (*De Sacramento*) as the third book,[3] though it has a history of circulating as a stand-alone text on the Eucharist.[4] For this reason it seems right to treat it in depth by itself.

As mentioned previously, Thomas is often dependent on Augustine of Hippo and no less so for his theology of grace. Viewed most simply, grace concerns the relation between God and his creation, especially humankind. By grace, God demonstrates his love and saving nature to his creatures and demonstrates his favor through his act of deliverance in Jesus Christ. In the New Testament, grace is understood to be God's free and loving turning to sinners in the atoning death of Jesus Christ: the believer is "justified by his grace as a gift, through the redemption that is in Christ Jesus" (Rom 3:24). God's saving actions are a gift of grace: "For by grace you have been saved through faith. And this is not your own doing; it is the gift of God, not a result of works, so that no one may boast" (Eph 2:8–9). Building on this, the primary understanding of grace in Augustine's theology "refers to that divine operation in angels and humans through which they are moved to know and love God."[5] In the words of Augustine, "For we must understand the grace of God through Jesus Christ our Lord. It alone sets human beings free from evil, and without it they do

---

Augustine is when he quotes the bishop of Hippo's famous aphorism, "you have made us for yourself, and our heart is restless until it rests in you" (Augustine of Hippo, *Confessions* I.1.1; Chadwick, trans., *Saint Augustine: Confessions*, 3). Thomas writes, "For my heart cannot rest nor be wholly content until it rests in you" (4.21; 121).

3. Ruelens, *The Imitation of Christ*, 7.
4. Post, *The Modern Devotion*, 523.
5. Burns, "Grace," 391.

nothing good whether in thinking, in willing and loving, or in acting. Grace not merely teaches them so that they know what they should do, but also grants that they do with love what they know."[6] Also, for Augustine, grace is not a created disposition or accident but an operation and indwelling of God within the created order. Grace is marked by God's presence and power in the created world upon which all creatures depend. Without grace "creation would lapse into immobility and nothingness."[7]

From his reading of the Scriptures Augustine came to see that this divine operation, or grace, took two forms in the angels and humans: light in the mind and love in the will. The light is identified with the Word of God, which guides creaturely understanding and judgment: "Through the prophets, apostles, preachers, and the Scriptures, and even incarnated in humanity, the Word guides sinners toward the inner perception of divine Truth."[8] Love, for Augustine, is synonymous with the Holy Spirit, who is the divine love that is God and from God.[9] Love moves believers "to appreciate and desire God above everything else and to love self, neighbor, and all lower goods for the sake of God's goodness."[10] In short, for Augustine "Grace is fundamentally the illumination of the mind by divine Truth, the Word of God, and the movement of the will by divine Love, the Holy Spirit. This divine operation [or grace] takes many forms, which are differentiated by the condition of

6. Augustine of Hippo, *Rebuke and Grace* 3; Teske, trans., *Answer to the Pelagians, IV*, 110.

7. Burns, "Grace," 392.

8. Burns, "Grace," 392.

9. On medieval conceptions of the Holy Spirit as Love, see Peter Lombard, *Sentences* 1.X.1 and Dante Alighieri, *Paradisio* 10.1–3; 13.52–57; and 13.79–81.

10. Burns, "Grace," 393.

the particular created spirit: repentance, faith, prayer, charity, perseverance, and glory." Thus, "God works in many ways, from governance of the bodily world, through control of the effects of good and evil intentions, to dwelling and operating within the good angels and faithful Christians."[11]

By the high Middle Ages grace was often understood to be a substance, a *res* (a "thing") that was available to all through a means of grace (e.g., the sacraments). Once obtained, this grace was effectual to the end for which it was intended; that is, it worked *ex opere operato* ("from the work worked") so that the grace received did the work that it was intended to do assuming the recipient obtained it with the proper moral condition. For Thomas Aquinas (d. 1274), the world was imbued with God's grace as a result of its divine creation; therefore, not every human action needs additional grace. All human actions, he writes, "whether corporal or spiritual, derive from the absolute prime mover, which is God."[12] Further, "Human nature is not so corrupted by sin . . . as to be deprived of natural good altogether."[13] Humans are able to do some good simply by being created by God. Yet, "in the state of pure nature man [*sic*] needs a power added to his natural power by grace, for one reason, namely, in order to do and to will supernatural grace."[14] A person cannot, then, be redeemed apart from a divinely added supernatural grace and even the believer's response to this superadded grace is an act of grace: "a man cannot prepare himself for grace without the help of grace.

---

11. Burns, "Grace," 398.

12. Thomas Aquinas, *Summa Theologiae* 1a2ae, q. 109, art. 1; Fairweather, trans., *Nature and Grace*, 138.

13. Thomas Aquinas, *Summa Theologiae* 1a2ae, q. 109, art. 2; Fairweather, trans., *Nature and Grace*, 140.

14. Thomas Aquinas, *Summa Theologiae* 1a2ae, q. 109, art. 2; Fairweather, trans., *Nature and Grace*, 141.

... A man cannot therefore turn to God except through God turning him to himself."[15] Thus, for Aquinas, and for the thirteenth-century church in general, humankind is in desperate need of God's grace and assistance, both to be saved and to progress in holiness, for the "help of grace is ... indispensable if a man [sic] is to rise from sin."[16] This necessary grace comes through the sacraments, for "Sacraments are necessary for human salvation,"[17] especially the Holy Eucharist, because it is the greatest of all the sacraments.[18]

The centrality of the Holy Eucharist in the life of the high and late medieval church is evidenced by the institution of the feast of Corpus Christi. This Eucharistic feast originated in the thirteenth century under the inspiration of the Belgian Juliana of Cornillon (d. 1258),[19] who was an orphan educated by Augustinian nuns. In time she took religious vows with the same community and later became superior of the community. Juliana was devoted to the blessed sacrament and wished for a feast in its honor, a desire she communicated to Robert of Thourotte, the bishop of Liège. Favorably inclined, he called a synod in 1246 at which he ordered that a Corpus Christi celebration be held the following year.[20] An Office for Corpus Christi was drawn up and the feast was celebrated for the first time by the canons

15. Thomas Aquinas, *Summa Theologiae* 1a2ae, q. 109, art. 6; Fairweather, trans., *Nature and Grace*, 147–8.

16. Thomas Aquinas, *Summa Theologiae* 1a2ae, q. 109, art. 7; Fairweather, trans., *Nature and Grace*, 149–50.

17. Thomas Aquinas, *Summa Theologiae* 3, q. 61, art. 1; Bauerschmidt, *Holy Teaching*, 254.

18. Thomas Aquinas, *Summa Theologiae* 3, q. 65, art. 3.

19. For the *vita* of Juliana see Mulder-Bakker, ed., *Living Saints of the Thirteenth Century*, 181–297.

20. For Robert's letter to the clergy in Liège establishing the feast, see Mulder-Bakker, ed., *Living Saints of the Thirteenth Century*, 300–302.

of St. Martin at Liège. Providentially, Jacques Pantaléon, the former archdeacon of Liège, was elected pope in August 1261, taking the name Urban IV. Henry of Guelders, the new bishop of Liège, at the request of a recluse named Eve, asked the pope to extend the celebration to the entire world.[21] Pope Urban responded to the request of the bishop of Liège by publishing the bull *Transiturus de hoc mundo* on August 11, 1264 in which he ordered the annual celebration of Corpus Christi on the Thursday after Trinity Sunday (i.e., during the second week of Pentecost).

Interestingly, as noted in chapter 3, Thomas entered the community of Mt. St. Agnes on the Feast of Corpus Christi: "In the year of the Lord 1406, on the Feast of Corpus Christi . . . two brothers that were Clerks, and one that was a Convert, were invested. These were Thomas Hemerken of the city of Kempen . . . [and] Oetbert Wilde of Zwolle."[22] By this time celebration of Corpus Christi was common throughout the Latin church, including at Mt. St. Agnes.[23] As well, at least some women's communities of the Windesheim Congregation constructed their church so that the nun's choir had an unobstructed view of the main altar, "allowing the canonesses to see the host during the Elevation" yet "without being seen. . . . Only small windows were built in so that the canonesses were able to see the elevation of the host during the Mass, the central focus of

---

21. A translation of the pope's letter of response to Eve is found in Mulder-Bakker, ed., *Living Saints of the Thirteenth Century*, 298-300.

22. Thomas à Kempis, *Chronicle* 10; Arthur, trans., *The Chronicle of the Canons*, 41.

23. The *liber ordinarius* of Mt. St. Agnes (copied in 1456) provides detailed information on how the monastery organized liturgical celebrations, including the Corpus Christi procession, evidence of its observance in the monastery. See Louviot, "Controlling Space, Disciplining Voice," 105, 156 and Appendix 5.

the celebration."[24] Given this centrality of Eucharistic practice and observance, it is not surprising, then, that Thomas would devote a whole book to the blessed sacrament.

Before looking at the *Imitatio* itself it should be noted that the interiority of devotion presented by Thomas in regard to the Holy Eucharist stands in tension with the visual components of devotion vis-à-vis the feast of Corpus Christi. Whereas the consecrated Host was paraded about in a Corpus Christi procession for all to see and venerate, Thomas advocated for an interior and invisible reverence. Maximillian van Habsburg goes so far as to conclude that the "*Imitatio* was reacting against the excessive importance attached to the visual elements of devotion in order to direct the emphasis towards inward contemplation, . . . though the tangible forms of Eucharistic devotion were not denounced in the *Imitatio*."[25] For Thomas, the Holy Eucharist was both an outward and an inward devotion and all that it accomplished was due to the grace of God.

---

24. Louviot, "Controlling Space, Disciplining Voice," 128. By the high Middle Ages the focal point and whole reason to attend a Mass for most people was to see the elevated Host. By the end of the twelfth century, the priest at the altar had begun to elevate the host for all to see just after the sacring (i.e., consecration); that is, just after saying the words of institution—"This is my body." In time, this action was accompanied by the ringing of a bell so that those present would abandon their private prayers to look up. This was necessary given the fact that much of what the priest said, including the words of institution, were inaudible or unintelligible (because they were spoken in Latin) to those present.

25. Von Habsburg, *Catholic and Protestant Translations of the Imitatio Christi*, 27.

GRACE IN THE IMITATION OF CHRIST (BOOKS 1, 2, AND 4)

Thomas has a lot to say about grace throughout the *Imitation* but particularly in Book 4.53–55, which serve as a mini-treatise on grace. Any discussion of grace in Thomas must begin here. Grace is precious and undeserved (4.40), says Thomas, therefore it cannot be mixed with worldly things nor will it come to the one who is not rightly prepared for it. "Therefore," he writes, "if you wish to receive it, you must remove every obstacle to grace" (4.53; 167). The removal of obstacles include: seclusion and solitariness; silence; devout prayer; contempt of the world; putting God first place in one's life over "outward things"; detachment from friends and family; and independence "of this world's consolations." In short, adopting the posture of a stranger and pilgrim to the world prepares one for grace. Weak-souled people are unable to do this, says Thomas, but only those whose "passions are subject to his reason, and his reason wholly subject to" God can make progress in this way. Yet, this is only the beginning, believes Thomas, not the end. This "brave beginning" cuts out and destroys "all inordinate and secret love of self, and of any personal and material advantage" (4.53; 168). Does this mean that the believer who hopes to receive grace needs to earn that right? Is this not just a form of works-based righteousness? No, given Thomas' distinction between nature and grace.

As one contemporary scholar rightly notes, "the topic of nature and grace touches almost any and every theological and even human question, for one's appraisal of this issue transforms the way in which one understands the very encounter between man [sic] and God."[26] Similarly, "No Christian doctrine can be dealt with adequately without

26. Swafford, *Nature and Grace*, 1.

recourse to the nature and grace schema."[27] At bare minimum, the phrase "nature and grace" has two aspects: 1) that Christ is the center and end of all things; and 2) "the necessity of distinguishing between nature and grace for the purpose of preserving the supernatural transcendence and gratuity of grace."[28] The first understanding is found in two biblical texts: "For by [Christ] all things were created, in heaven and on earth, visible and invisible, whether thrones or dominions or rulers or authorities—all things were created through him and for him. And he is before all things, and in him all things hold together" (Col 1:16–17); and, "making known to us the mystery of his will, according to his purpose, which he set forth in Christ as a plan for the fullness of time, to unite all things in him, things in heaven and things on earth" (Eph 1:9–10). The latter understanding is reflected strongly in the writings of Augustine of Hippo, especially in his treatise *Nature and Grace*, which he wrote around 415 against Pelagius.[29]

Augustine sums up his teachings on nature and grace in this way: 1) human nature was created blameless, without defect; 2) but now human nature born of Adam needs a physician; 3) this defect is not from God, the blameless maker of humankind, but it "came from the original sin which was committed by free choice"[30]; thus, 4) God's punishment for sin is absolutely just. The medicine to cure

27. Carpenter, *Nature and Grace*, ix.

28. Swafford, *Nature and Grace*, 1.

29. Pelagius was likely a Briton by birth who arrived in Rome ca. 380. His views on human nature came to be seen as heretical and his thought was a frequent target for Augustine. In short, Pelagius believed that human nature was such that a person could chose to obey the commandments of God; that is, sin was not inevitable. Pelagius ended his life in the East (possibly Egypt), dying sometime after 418.

30. Augustine of Hippo, *Nature and Grace* 3.3; Teske, trans., *Answer to the Pelagians*, 226.

sinful humankind is grace and it is a free gift of God. Those who do not receive God's grace, for any reason, cannot be redeemed and are condemned. Again, this grace is not merited but comes from God's mercy for "he sets free those whom he will."[31] Yet again, Thomas would fully agree with Augustine.

Thomas believes that nature and grace "are opposed to one another" yet they work so subtly together that they can hardly be distinguished, even by "holy and enlightened" persons.[32] Though each person desires to do what is good, she is deceived into thinking that she is, in fact, virtuous. This leads Thomas into eight paragraphs, structured in the same way ("Nature is . . . but grace is . . ."), that make it possible to tell the difference between nature and grace. He concludes with two paragraphs that simply affirm what grace is and what it does. First, nature "is crafty, and seduces many, snaring and deceiving, . . . and always works for her own ends." Grace, on the other hand, is simple and honest, doing "all things purely for love God, in whom she rests as her final goal." Second, nature resists mortification and control whereas grace "mortifies herself, . . . seeks to be overcome, . . . [and] loves to be under discipline." Third, nature is only concerned with her own interests and what she can gain from others whereas grace only considers what is good for others. Further, nature wants honor and glory, fears shame and loves ease and comfort. Grace gives all honor and glory to God, is happy to suffer reproach, and "cannot be idle." Fourth, nature loves fancy things of this world but grace likes what is simple and humble and not of this world. Fifth, nature is greedy and "inclines a man [*sic*]

---

31. Augustine of Hippo, *Nature and Grace* 5.5; Teske, trans., *Answer to the Pelagians*, 227.

32. In this paragraph all quotations come from *Imitation* 4.54; 168–71.

towards creatures" (e.g., the body, vanities, and restlessness) so as to "gratify the senses," but grace draws people towards God and virtue by fleeing the world, seeking comfort in God alone and delighting in God above all visible things. Sixth, nature "does everything for her own gain and interest," but grace "seeks no worldly return, and asks for no reward, but God alone." Seventh, nature likes to hang around with powerful and rich people, but grace is satisfied with the company of her enemies, the poor and other honest persons. Eighth, nature hates hardship, but grace "bears poverty with courage." Nature is egotistical, but grace is God-focused. Nature is curious, wanting to know secrets and gossip whereas grace submits her knowing powers to God, discerning that "there is nothing new or lasting in this world."[33]

From this, Thomas concludes that grace "teaches us how the senses are to be disciplined and vain complacency avoided; how anything likely to excite praise and admiration should be humbly concealed; and how in all things and in all knowledge some useful fruit should be sought, together with the praise and honour of God." But it is the final paragraph of 4.54 that provides Thomas' clearest definition of grace: "Grace is a supernatural light, and the especial gift of God, the seal of His chosen and the pledge of [eternal] salvation, which raises man [sic] from earthly things to love the heavenly [*de terrenis ad cœlestia amanda sustollit*], and from worldly makes him spiritual [*de carnali spiritualem efficit*]." Grace, then, is absolutely necessary for a devout person to progress from a worldly person to a spiritual person. There is no room for works-righteousness in Thomas'

---

33. A ninth distinction is found at 4.31; 137: "Nature regards the outward characteristics of a man [sic]: Grace considers [*convertit* = converts] his inner disposition. And while Nature is often misled, Grace trusts in God and cannot be deceived."

theology. By grace nature "is controlled and overcome" so that more grace can be given,[34] but the whole "process" is one of grace; that is, it begins and ends with grace.[35] As the disciple prays, "Lord, make possible for me by grace what is impossible to me by nature" (4.19; 118).

In the final chapter that makes up the mini-treatise on grace (4.55), Thomas turns his attention to nature's corruption and grace's power.[36] Though created in the image and likeness of God, there are, says Thomas, "base elements" (*pessimam*) of human nature. It is these elements that drag the devout person down into sin. But what are these "base elements"? More or less these "base elements" are the evil intentions in fallen human beings. Augustine describes the rebellious Israelites has having a "wicked desire"[37] (*cupiditatem pessimam*; see Num 11:4) and elsewhere describes heretics as part of an "evil generation" (*pessimam generationem*).[38] For Thomas, these "base elements" drag the devout person "down into sin and perdition." These "base elements" contend against one's mind and can lead "to all kinds of sensuality" were it not for the grace of God (cf. 1.1; 28). Thomas confesses that he could not resist these "base

---

34. See also, for example, 1.25; 64: "the more completely a man overcomes and cleanses himself in spirit, the more he profits and deserves abundant grace"; and 4.9; 105: "they who freely and willingly serve Me, shall receive grace upon grace."

35. See 4.49; 159 where Thomas asserts that the devout person's desire for eternal blessedness is of heavenly origin that "is not by any resolution or effort of your own . . . but solely by the favour and grace of Heaven and God's regard."

36. In this paragraph all quotations come from *Imitation* 4.55; 171-73.

37. Augustine of Hippo, *On Christian Teaching* 11.46; Green, trans., *Saint Augustine: On Christian Teaching*, 133.

38. Augustine of Hippo, *Literal Meaning of Genesis* 11.25.32; Hill, trans., *On Genesis*, 447.

elements" except God's "most holy grace is poured glowing into my heart to help me." Without the grace of God nature cannot be subdued since it is now fallen "through Adam" and "tainted by sin." It is sin that makes each person tend toward evil and base things. Fallen human proclivity to sin is not part of humankind's original nature. There is, writes Thomas, a residual goodness in all humans because human nature was originally created good:

> The little strength that remains is only like a small spark, buried beneath ashes. Yet this same natural reason, though hidden in profound darkness, still retains the power to know good and evil, and to discern truth and falsehood. But it is powerless to do what it knows to be good, neither does it enjoy the full light of truth, nor its former healthy affections.

Thomas continues by acknowledging his ability, as one created in the image and likeness of God, to delight in God's law and to know God's commandments. Nonetheless, he serves the law of sin, fails to follow his reason, and is powerless to exercise his will to do good without the grace of God: "Lord, how urgently I need Your grace if I am to undertake, carry out and perfect any good work! Without it, I can achieve nothing; but in You and by the power of Your grace, all things are possible."

Thomas continues by noting that nothing in and of itself is of much value unless it be "allied to grace." Thomas acknowledges that the world of nature is imbued with divine goodness and is, thereby, common to both good and bad people. But grace is God's special gift to those whom he chooses and is, thereby, supernatural. Grace takes was is ordinary, what is natural, and makes it acceptable to God, for even faith or hope without grace is unpleasing to God, says Thomas. Grace takes what is natural and elevates it to the supernatural, including his chosen people: "Without grace, I am nothing," writes Thomas, "but a dry tree, a barren stock fit only for destruction." In Thomas' theology God gives his grace generously to all who ask and to all who are worthy so that it will make the devout person "more humble, more reverent, and more ready to renounce self" (2.10; 81). In short, the grace of Christ effects "great things in the frail frame of man [sic]" (2.12; 87) therefore all disciples ought to put their trust in God's gift of grace (4.7; 101).

At the same time, it is also important to note that despite the absolute necessity of grace in Thomas' theology, he also thinks that God's grace can be withdrawn. God's grace may be a gift but it is one that can be withdrawn by the Giver (e.g., 4.13). In 2.9, Thomas reminds his readers that joy and devotion come when God imparts his grace, bestowing spiritual comfort and consolation. This bestowal of grace is from God and he does it freely, not based on any merit in a person. Moreover, not only is God the one who grants this grace but he is also the one who can, and does at times, remove it. For example, King David received God's grace, but it was withdrawn for a season. Thomas says that these seasons of desolation, apart from the grace of God, are "the experience of great Saints" and no one, no matter how religious and devout, is immune, so how much the more those who "are sometimes fervent and sometimes cold of heart." This leads Thomas to exclaim,

> In what, then, can I place my hope or trust, save in the great mercy of God alone, and in the hope of His heavenly grace? For whether I enjoy the company of good men, or devout Brethren, or faithful friends; whether holy books, beautiful treatises, or sweet singing and hymns; all these are of little help or comfort when I am forsaken by grace and left to my own poverty.

But God does not utterly forsake those whom he loves so grace always returns (4.21 and 57).

In the end, Thomas' theology of grace is rather traditional, at least in the Augustinian sense. Grace comes from God so that the devout follower of Christ can be helped (1.25), refreshed (1.18), and strengthened (2.8) to do the works that God calls her to do. Grace is unmerited but comes to those who ask (4.15), assuming all obstacles to its reception have been removed (4.53). And grace is not just for the weak but for the saints of God too, coming not only directly from God's Holy Spirit (4.27) but also from participation in the Holy Eucharist.

ON THE BLESSED SACRAMENT

As is true of the *Imitation* as a whole, the chapters of Book 3, "On the Blessed Sacrament" (or, more fully, "A devout exhortation to the Holy Communion of Christ's body"), do not appear to have a clear thematic arrangement. If there was one it is known only to Thomas. Therefore, I will treat each chapter successively, working through the topics as presented in the printed edition of the *Imitation*, but before beginning it should be noted that the book is written, like Book 4, as a dialogue between Christ and "the disciple." At times the teaching comes from the disciple and at other times from Christ himself.

The first teaching on receiving the Eucharist reverently comes from the disciple, whose knowledge of his sin restrains him from receiving the sacrament. He understands that as a person of faith he can approach and "have part" in Christ, but he finds greater consolation in Jesus' invitation to "Come to me ... and I will refresh you" (Matt 11:28). Nonetheless, the disciple questions how he, so generally unprepared, could come into God's presence by way of the sacrament since he is rarely fully recollected and free from distraction, prerequisites for proper reception. Such dread in approaching the Eucharist is rooted in the belief that the body of Christ has "ineffable powers" (*ineffabilibus virtutibus*) and that it fulfills "all the ancient rites"; that is, it is the consummation of all the promises and commandments of the old covenant. If King David danced before the Ark of God then "how much greater devotion and reverence should . . . all Christian people have in the presence of the Sacrament." Furthermore, Thomas confesses that Christ is "wholly present" in the sacrament, therefore it can only be eaten with faith, hope, and love. In receiving, the worthy communicant receives "the grace of devotion," "hidden grace," and "spiritual grace" that restores virtue to the soul and renews its "sin-ravaged beauty" (3.1; 186). Because of the grace conveyed in the sacrament it strengthens soul, mind, and body.

Thomas continues by lamenting how unworthily devout persons receive the sacrament due to carelessness, tepidity, blindness, and hard-heartedness. Though outside of religious communities there was infrequent reception of the Eucharistic, Thomas warns that frequent reception may cause a loss of reverence.[39] He imagines that if Holy Communion were celebrated in one place only by one priest alone then everyone would flock "to be present at the divine mysteries." So how much more amazing is it that Christ is

---

39. Already at Lateran IV in 1215 the church's bishops and theologians admonished everyone to receive the sacrament of the Holy Eucharist at least once a year: "All the faithful of both sexes shall, after they have reached the age of reason, faithfully confess all their sins at least once a year to their own priest and perform to the best of their ability the penance imposed, receiving reverently, at least at Easter, the sacrament of the Eucharist" (Tanner, ed., *Decrees of the Ecumenical Councils, Volume I*, 245). Nonetheless, infrequent communion remained the norm.

offered in many places so that "Holy Communion is diffused through the world" (3.1; 187). Christ is present in the Holy Eucharist, grace comes by way of the Holy Eucharist, and its availability is everywhere, therefore devout men and women need to prepare themselves appropriately and receive communion worthily and frequently.

In the next chapter, Thomas continues lamenting his sin and lowliness while at the same time extolling and praising God for his goodness. All praise is due to God for condescending to make himself available in the sacrament. Thomas continues theologizing about Christ's real presence in the bread and the wine by saying that this "Food is none other than Yourself" (3.2; 188) and "You give Yourself to be our food" (3.2; 189). And by this real, corporeal presence Thomas is in keeping with the medieval church's position that Christ's presence would of necessity be his *whole* self, since he is both fully God and fully human. Orthodox Christian theology, codified in the fourth century's Nicene-Constantinopolitan Creed, confesses that Jesus Christ was (and is) fully divine while also simultaneously being fully human and that this remains true even after his resurrection and ascension to God the Father in heaven.[40] In consequence, Christ's presence in the Eucharistic bread and wine would mean that he is there as *both* fully God *and* fully human: "true God and true man, are wholly present under the simple forms of bread and wine, and are eaten without being consumed."[41] This means that he who receives the body

40. Theologically this union of God and man is referred to as the hypostatic union. That is, that Christ's two *hypostases* (or, in Latin, *persona*) are united in the one person of Jesus Christ so that he is the God-man. Why this is Christologically and soteriologically necessary is worked out, in particular, by Anselm of Canterbury (d. 1093) in his *Cur Deus Homo*.

41. See also 3.3; 191: you "stoop to visit the poor and humble soul, and to satisfy her hunger with Your whole Divinity and Humanity [*sic*]."

and blood of Christ is a "sharer in all the merits of Christ." But for a priest, like Thomas, it also means that he needs to celebrate the Eucharist "with a glad and pure conscience" and "Whenever you celebrate or hear Mass, it should be as great and as joyful to you as if on this very day Christ had come down for the first time" (3.2; 189).

Having lamented the bad practice of receiving (somewhat) unworthily and infrequently and having established that Christ is wholly present in the bread and wine, Thomas is now in a position to argue for frequent communion, in part because of the many blessings that come from partaking of the Holy Eucharist. Thomas acknowledges that only God can satisfy. In Augustinian language, which Thomas appropriates, "For my heart cannot rest nor be wholly content until it rests in You" (4.21; 121).[42] Further, humankind is sin-sick and needs "the medicine of salvation." The heavenly food of the Eucharist is this "remedy" and is so effective at eradicating the sickness that it not only restores the devout believer to health but it makes it possible for "whoever receives . . . worthily . . . [to] be a partaker and heir of eternal glory" (3.3; 190; see 2 Pet 1:4). The medicine of Eucharistic grace renews, cleanses, and enkindles the sick sinner. In overt theological terms: "Holy Communion both restrains man [sic] from evil, and establishes him in goodness" (3.3; 191), for "this most high and venerable Sacrament is the health of soul and body, the cure of every spiritual malady" (3.4; 192).[43] This restoration to health allows one to taste the sweetness of God's goodness[44] and the grace received thereby makes it possible for the

---

42. See Augustine of Hippo, *Confessions* 1.1.1.

43. The medicinal language of healing is also used by Thomas in 3.10.

44. Holy Communion itself is the "Fount of sweetness" (3.4; 193).

communicant to give herself to devotion[45] and to prepare her heart to "obtain a portion of the divine fire" (3.4; 193). The health that comes by way of Holy Communion not only restores the disciple to his natural health but configures him supernaturally.

Having mentioned the place of priests vis-à-vis the Holy Eucharist in passing already, in 3.5 Thomas turns his attention directly to the priestly office. Consistent with medieval belief and practice, Thomas holds the priesthood in high esteem: "High the office, and great the dignity of a priest."[46] And elsewhere: "how high and honourable is the office of priests, to whom is given power to consecrate with sacred words the Lord of majesty, to bless Him with their lips, to hold Him in their hands, to receive Him in their mouths, and to communicate Him to others" (3.11; 206). Nonetheless, no man is worthy of this office much less has a man merited it. But once someone has been made a priest by the imposition of a bishop's hands then he, and only he, has a right and the power, as an ordained priest, "to hallow the Body of Christ," though this is done by using the words of God with "God himself" as "the principal agent and unseen worker" (3.5; 194). Because the priest sacramentally "occupies the place of Christ" (*Christi vices gerit*)[47] he must be virtuous and an example to others. He must also be eager to celebrate the Eucharist "faithfully, regularly and devoutly" for that is why he has been ordained, honoring God and edifying the church by so doing (3.5; 195). And he must also be fully and properly prepared to serve at God's

---

45. Cf. 3.4; 194: "grant that through the reception of Your mysteries the fire of devotion may kindle in me."

46. See Peters and Anderson, eds., *A Companion to Priesthood and Holy Orders in the Middle Ages*.

47. Historically theologians have expressed this idea by the Latin phrase *in persona Christi* (in the person of Christ).

altar (3.7). First, a priest must engage in self-examination so that he can identify his sins, grieve for them, and confess them to God, cleansing and purifying himself thereby. Second, having identified his sins, the priest resolves to amend his life and to progress in holiness, offering himself on the altar of his heart[48] and committing himself to God so that he may worthily approach the altar of God.[49]

Having examined himself and repented, the priest is now able to offer Christ both sacramentally on the altar and to the people of God in Holy Communion. In these offerings, however, the priest is not offering Christ anew since Christ has already offered himself freely to God. Thomas says that the priest's main offering to God is himself, for God does not seek a "gift, but yourself" (3.8; 198). Thomas believes that Christ gave himself on the altar of the cross at his crucifixion and gives himself on the Eucharistic altar so that the priest will give himself back to Christ. In short, this is a loss of oneself in order to be wholly united to God. This is the Eucharistic mystery for Thomas—that a priest's offering of himself is intimately joined to Christ's self-offering at Calvary so that thus united the bread and the wine will become, through the priest's ritual actions, the body and blood of Jesus Christ. Only in this way is the priest's offering acceptable to God. Furthermore, the priest's offering of himself to God, joined to Jesus' self-offering, avails for the

---

48. The concept of the "altar of the heart" goes back to the patristic era. Particularly relevant to Thomas' thought is Augustine of Hippo's comment that "We offer to Him upon the altar of our hearts the sacrifice of humility and praise, kindled by the fire of love" (*City of God* 10.3; Dyson, trans., *Augustine: The City of God*, 395).

49. On proper preparation for receiving the sacrament see also 3.6 and 12. In 3.12 Thomas helpfully, and rightly, notes that there is also the need to guard oneself and to foster devotion *after* receiving Communion just as much as there is to prepare oneself in advance.

salvation of God's people and for the "holy aspirations of devout persons" (3.9; 200).

Given the salvific nature of the blessed sacrament, it must not be lightly forgone. Because he knows the value of the Eucharist for devout persons, Satan actively attempts to discourage and prevent reception of Holy Communion, especially among those who are intentionally preparing to receive it. As well, devout people "are often hindered by an undue concern about devout feelings, and by anxieties about confession" (3.10; 201). Though one does not want to communicate unworthily there is the need to end one's preparation in order to receive lest one be accused of scrupulosity, which is an obstacle to God's grace and extinguishes devotion. Heeding the advice of a spiritual director, the devout woman should "not postpone receiving Communion for every little worry and doubt" but should trust in the veracity and efficacy of her pre-Communion confession as well-preparing her to commune. Daily difficulties are a fact of life and must not be deterrents to eager and proper reception. As importantly, delaying Communion will inevitably lead to sloth and spiritual dryness. Thomas refers to those who put off Communion as "half-hearted and careless people" (3.10; 202) because they do not want to do the hard work of preparing themselves properly. But blessed is the devout person who is eager and prepared to commune daily and so is the one who is "avoidably prevented." The sincere communicant, even if he is prevented from communing, is rewarded for his desire but also encouraged to make a spiritual communion with Christ, though it is never a substitute for the "mystic communion and spiritual refreshment" (*mystice communicat et invisibiliter*) of the Holy Eucharist (3.10; 203).[50]

50. The concept of "spiritual communion" is rooted in Thomas Aquinas' distinction between eating Christ sacramentally or

Though the Holy Eucharist held pride of place in medieval pastoral practice, it was not to the exclusion of preaching. For example, at Lateran IV the council fathers decreed, "Among other things that pertain to the salvation of the Christian people, the food of the word of God is above all necessary, because as the body is nourished by material food, so is the soul nourished by spiritual food since 'not by bread alone does the human person live, but by every word that comes from the mouth of God' (Mt 4:4)."[51] Thomas, therefore, rightly yokes the Eucharist to preaching. He notes that one day, in eternal glory, there will be no need for Holy Communion because the glorified saints will "taste the Word of God made man, as He was from the beginning, and as He abides eternally" (3.11; 204). That is, one does not need Christ in the bread and the wine when one is in the presence of the flesh-and-blood Christ. Though all things will find their full and final consummation eschatologically, until then there is the ongoing need for the devout person to be strengthened by the example of the saints, comforted by the Holy Scriptures, and made healthy by the holy body and blood of the Eucharist. In short, Thomas says that believers have two needs: food and light. Food comes in Holy Communion and light comes from the Scriptures "for the Word of God is the light of my soul, and Your Sacrament is the bread of my life" (3.11; 205).

In the last chapters of Book 3, especially 13–16, Thomas circles around again to themes that he has expressed elsewhere in Book 3. One place, however, where

---

spiritually in the Holy Eucharist. When eating spiritually the believer is desiring and yearning for the sacrament in a spiritual manner because, for some reason, he is prohibited from sacramentally eating the bread and wine. Thus, this spiritual eating constitutes a "spiritual communion," though Thomas Aquinas does not use this exact phrase. See Thomas Aquinas, *Summa Theologiae* 3, q. 80, arts. 1 and 11.

51. Tanner, ed., *Decrees of the Ecumenical Councils, Volume I*, 239.

he offers something new is in his discussion of how the Holy Eucharist brings union between the communicant and Christ. Thomas expresses the desire to withdraw from created things so that he may be "wholly united" to Christ. This, he says, is aided through frequent reception of Holy Communion and, because he is a priest, frequent celebration of the Holy Eucharist. These will enable him to "delight in heavenly and eternal things more and more" and will make it possible for his soul to dwell in Christ (3.13; 209). Through the grace that comes from the sacrament the devout person's soul is elevated (3.13: *cor erigendum in cælum*) and enlarged (3.15: *dilatabitur cor*) so that as "he receives the sacred Eucharist, he merits the great grace of divine union" (3.15; 213). In a stirring passage, the disciple prays to this end: "Oh, that You would set me wholly afire by Your presence, and change [*transmutes*] me into Yourself, that I might be made one spirit with You by the grace of inward vision, and by the fusion of ardent love" (3.16; 213–14). In this request, so pregnant with redolent imagery, the devout believer asks God to transubstantiate him, if you will, into a little Christ in the same way that the bread and wine are transubstantiated in the Mass into the body and blood of Christ. That is to say, the disciple views union in such ontological terms that he wants to become Christ himself. But then, in another evocative passage, Thomas changes the language and asks God to make him into another Virgin Mary because she "desired and received You" devoutly and humbly or into a John the Baptist who leapt for joy in the presence of Christ (3.17; 214–15). If he cannot become a little Christ, Thomas desires to be another Mary or John the Baptist.

Thomas ends his treatise on the blessed sacrament by emphasizing the mysterious nature of the Holy Eucharist; that is, that it is a mystery that must be believed humbly, not necessarily only intellectually or logically. A "curious and unprofitable inquiry into the Mysteries" can lead to doubt since its fullness is beyond comprehension. In fact, some believers "have lost their devotion by attempting to pry into matters too high for them." Therefore, "faith and holy life are required of you, not a lofty intellect or knowledge of the profound mysteries of God" (3.18; 216). Reason is humbled before faith so that one can come to the sacrament faithfully and "with humble reverence, confidently committing to almighty God whatever you are not able to understand" (3.18; 217). In other words, proper reception of the blessed sacrament is by faith not by complete understanding. How Christ if wholly present in the bread and the wine, both as fully man and fully God, is beyond human comprehension and must remain a mystery to be marveled at, not domesticated.

CONCLUSION

In many ways Thomas' treatise on the blessed sacrament is typically medieval in that it does not move Eucharistic theology forward. Its focus is not on explaining or making fully intelligible the mystery that is the Eucharist, which is ultimately inscrutable anyway, but on receiving Christ in the bread and the wine.[52] Thomas' concern, which is consistent with the whole *Imitation*, is that the communicant's inner disposition is such that he is communing worthily and

52. Notice, however, that Thomas mostly only mentions the bread as the body of Christ. This is because by the high Middle Ages communicants communed in one kind only; that is, they partook of the bread alone. The cup was withheld for multiple reasons and one of the central tenets of Protestant Eucharistic theology in the Reformation era was to offer the wine alongside the bread as normal Communion practice. On the history of this practice and medieval attempts to change it, see Patapios, "*Sub utraque specie.*"

Thomas' Spiritual Theology II

experiencing the plethora of benefits thereby. Thomas also recognizes the unique role and standing of the priest vis-à-vis the Holy Eucharist, but his main concern for the priest is that he too receive worthily. Following Rudolph Van Dijk's argument outlined in chapter 4 above, the whole point of the Eucharist is to bring about inner consolation (the topic of Book 4 in the original manuscript ordering). To that end, Thomas' Eucharistic theology is not an end itself but a means to another end—inward consolation.

Due to the sacrament's efficacy, it is only natural that Holy Communion would become a common practice in the religious/monastic orders of the Latin church and this is no less true of the Augustinian canons at Mt. St. Agnes. But it was not only seen as efficacious for each devout believer who partook of it with due worthiness and reverence. The efficacy of the blessed sacrament was also used in times of trouble. For example, on the Feast of the Assumption in 1467, the community's

> most beloved Father George took the Ciborium of the Venerable Sacrament from the altar with all reverence, and the whole body of members, going before him in procession round the cloister, sang the Response, "Felix namque." After they had returned to the choir, they bowed the knee before the Revered Sacrament which was placed upon the altar, and sang the Antiphon, "Media Vita," with the verse and the Collect proper to times of pestilence, for at this time the plague had begun both here and in many places.[53]

Such Eucharistic devotion was common in the late Middle Ages, so much so that historian Eamon Duffy writes, "The

---

53. Thomas à Kempis, *Chronicle* 29; Arthur, trans., *The Chronicle of the Canons*, 138.

liturgy lay at the heart of medieval religion, and the Mass lay at the heart of the liturgy."[54] For Christians in the Middle Ages, the Mass was the sacred action that reenacted Jesus Christ's self-giving on the hill of Calvary. With each Eucharist Christ was sacrificed for the good of the church and the world. The reception of his body and blood brought much-needed grace to the communicant so that she could be nourished and renewed in her own walk with God and so that the Christian community could walk together in faith and love and charity with God and with one another. Thomas knew this well, so he, without doubt or hesitation, commended frequent yet worthy reception of the blessed sacrament to anyone who desired to imitate Christ.

DISCUSSION QUESTIONS

1. Has Thomas à Kempis' view changed or shaped your understanding of grace? If so, how?
2. Why is the Holy Eucharist so critical to Thomas à Kempis' view of grace?
3. What is the relationship between the inner disposition and grace?
4. How does partaking in the Holy Eucharist allow one to imitate Christ?

---

54. Duffy, *The Stripping of the Altars*, 91.

6

THE ONGOING RELEVANCE OF THOMAS' SPIRITUALITY

AT SOME POINT IN the late twentieth or early twenty-first century it became fashionable to profess that one was "spiritual but not religious." In this formulation, "religious" was employed oftentimes with reference to institutions; that is, "I am spiritual but I am not interested in the institutional forms that have grown up around organized religion." From a Christian theological standpoint, such a sentiment appears odd and is, in fact, incoherent, for God established the foundations of the church, including its institutional form, before the foundations of the world (cf. Eph 1:3–10). Furthermore, that the Son of God humbled himself to become a man ensured the church would be an institution, for the incarnation of Jesus Christ is the foundation for the church as dispenser of the sacraments and the sacraments come by way of the institutional church. Moreover, the sentiment "spiritual but not religious" is often used in an unnecessarily dualistic manner. The "spiritual but not religious" group seems to believe, at least implicitly, that to be one precludes the other. If one is "spiritual" then one cannot also be "religious" and vice versa. Such a dichotomous perspective seems artificial and unnecessary.

What is meant by "spiritual" and "religious," of course, will vary from one spiritual-but-not-religious person to the next. The Barna Group, in a 2017 study, even showed that some of these people make no faith claims at all. In fact, 90 percent of those who assert no faith but claim to be "spiritual" identify as either atheist, agnostic, or unaffiliated.[1] This would seem to stretch the limits of the word "spiritual" to its breaking point, at least from a Christian theological standpoint, for inherent in the word "spirit" is the person of the Holy Spirit. As Walter Principe notes,

> For [the apostle] Paul, the "spirit" within the human person is all that is ordered, led, or influenced by the *Pneuma Theou* or *Spiritus Dei*, whereas *sarx* or *caro* or "flesh" is everything in a person that is opposed to this influence of the Spirit of God. Thus *caro* or "flesh" could be the person's mind or will or heart as much as or even more than the physical flesh or the body if the mind, will, or heart resist the influence of the Spirit. For Paul the opposition is not between the incorporeal or non-material and the corporeal and material, but between two ways of life. The "spiritual" person (*pneumatikos, spiritualis*) is one whose life is guided by the Spirit of God; the "carnal" person (*sarkikos, carnalis*) is one

---

1. https://www.barna.com/research/meet-spiritual-not-religious/. Accessed April 28, 2020.

The Ongoing Relevance of Thomas' Spirituality

> whose life is opposed to the working and guidance of the Spirit of God.[2]

Thus, from a Christian standpoint one *cannot* be spiritual without reference to the Holy Spirit, thus one cannot be a person of no faith and be "spiritual." Philip Sheldrake captures this well when he writes,

> Even if there is common ground between different faith traditions regarding the meaning of spirituality, that is, the development of the human capacity for self-transcendence in relation to the Absolute (however this is named), nevertheless the specifically Christian approach is increasingly related to theological themes rather than otherwise.[3]

Perhaps the same could be said about those of "no faith" traditions? For those with no faith who claim to be "spiritual," it would be more accurate to think of them as "carnal but not religious."

In any case, and without a doubt, Thomas à Kempis' *Imitation of Christ* is a work of Christian spirituality. In fact, Thomas is quite certain of the role of the Holy Spirit in the life of the devout believer. For example, it is the Holy Spirit who makes it possible to both hear and understand spiritual teachings and it is the Holy Spirit who animates the devout follower: "The teaching of Jesus far transcends all the teachings of the Saints, and whosoever has His spirit will discover concealed in it heavenly manna. But many people . . . feel little desire to follow it, because they lack the spirit of Christ" (1.1; 27).[4] Further, it is the Holy Spirit who animates

---

2. Principe, "Toward Defining Spirituality," 130.

3. Sheldrake, "What Is Spirituality?" 52.

4. Romans 8:9 confirms that the "Spirit of Christ" is the Holy Spirit: "You, however, are not in the flesh but in the Spirit, if in fact the

the devout believer to pursue the spiritual life: "Strengthen me, O Lord God, by the grace of Your Holy Spirit. Grant me inward power and strength" (4.27). In short, the *Imitation* is a spiritual work, a work of Christian spirituality. This may seem blatantly obvious to those who take up the book and read, but that alone gives the work an ongoing relevance.

Further, the work of the Holy Spirit in the lives of Christian believers varies from one person to another, from one practice to another, for "God works uniquely in the lives of individual believers. . . . Each believer experiences the unique work of the Holy Spirit in her life . . . [because] [n]o one pattern of [spiritual] formation fits every person and personality type."[5] It is worthwhile then to investigate the history of the Christian church in order to look for guides for one's own spiritual journey. And the best guides oftentimes are those written works that are, without doubt, works of spirituality (in the aforementioned full Christian sense of the word). God can and does use anything, of course, to form the life of a devout follower, but those works that are concerned explicitly with the Christian life, with the spiritual formation of the human person, seem especially apt to the task. Adherents of the Modern Devotion knew this well so they legislated the regular and ongoing reading of both the Holy Scriptures and other devotional books, including the *Imitation of Christ*, the sermons of Bernard of Clairvaux, Bonaventure's life of Christ, the meditations of Pseudo-Anselm, Ludolf of Saxony's life of Christ, and works by Henry Suso.[6] Concerning the reading of the

---

Spirit of God dwells in you. Anyone who does not have the Spirit of Christ does not belong to him." So when Thomas uses this language he is referencing the Holy Spirit.

5. Peters, "Historical Theology and Spiritual Formation," 203.

6. Van Engen, *Devotio moderna*, 8 and 25.

The Ongoing Relevance of Thomas' Spirituality

Holy Scriptures and other devotional literature among the Modern Devout, John Van Engen explains,

> To focus on the life and passion of Christ was to read the Gospel and the writings that explained and ordered it. The contemplative reading of holy writings, especially Holy Scripture, was prescribed for all brothers and sisters, who were expected additionally to make up a kind of "notebook" (*rapiaria*) of those passages they found most compelling. Here too the New Devout stood heirs to a long monastic tradition.[7]

Reading in this way is an aid to spiritual formation and reading those who have come before is an important element in this formation. That the *Imitation* is one of the most frequently translated and read spiritual works of the past suggests its ongoing relevance. The past can and should be read to great benefit, and this commends the *Imitation* for its ongoing significance.

A good example of this relevance and benefit of the *Imitation* is in the life of John Wesley (d. 1791), founder of Methodism. In 1766 Wesley published his *Plain Account of Christian Perfection* in which he gave "a plain and distinct account of the steps by which [he] was led, during a course of many years, to embrace the doctrine of Christian perfection."[8] In this work Wesley says that three authors in particular influenced his understanding of the spiritual life: Jeremy Taylor (d. 1667), William Law (d. 1761), and Thomas à Kempis. Wesley read the *Imitation* for the first time ca. 1725: "In the year 1726, I met with Kempis's *Christian's Pattern*."[9] This encounter left its mark:

7. Van Engen, *Devotio moderna*, 26.
8. Wesley, *A Plain Account of Christian Perfection*, 5.
9. Though he says it is 1726, in a letter to his mother Susanna dated May 28, 1725 Wesley mentions that Thomas was recommended

> The nature and extent of inward religion, the religion of the heart, now appeared to me in a stronger light than ever it had done before. I saw, that giving even all my life to God (supposing it possible to do this, and go no farther) would profit me nothing, unless I gave my heart, yea all my heart, to him. I saw, that "simplicity of intention, and purity of affection," one design in all we speak or do, and one desire ruling all our tempers, are indeed "the wings of the soul," without which she can never ascend to the mount of God.[10]

In fact, the mark was so pronounced that Wesley credits the *Imitation* in his full and final conversion at Aldersgate on May 24, 1738, the day in which he felt his "heart strangely warmed": "When I was about twenty-two, my father pressed me to enter into holy orders. At the same time, the providence of God directing me to Kempis's 'Christian Pattern,' I began to see, that true religion was seated in the heart, and that God's law extended to all our thoughts as well as words and actions."[11] In short, what Wesley received from his reading of Thomas was a profound understanding of the interiority of the Christian faith, the inner working of the Holy Spirit in the life of the devout believer. Though Wesley thought Thomas "too strict," he took "sensible comfort in reading him."[12] In the end, Wesley's life was profoundly changed due to reading past spiritual masters, especially the *Imitation*.

---

to him and already expresses, in the letter, his disagreements with the *Imitation*, so he must have read Thomas sometime in 1725. See his "Letter to Susanna Wesley," May 28, 1725 in Outler, ed., *Works*, 25:162–64.

10. Wesley, *A Plain Account of Christian Perfection*, 5–6.
11. Outler, ed., *Works*, 18:243.
12. Outler, ed., *Works*, 18:243.

The Ongoing Relevance of Thomas' Spirituality

But perhaps the most important justification for the ongoing relevance of the *Imitation* is that it overcomes the implicit yet false dichotomy in modern religious thinking between one's personal, albeit subjective, "spirituality" and an institution (e.g., the Roman Catholic Church or Orthodox Judaism). Though conceptions of the "self" were not unknown in antiquity and early Christian history, it was in the twelfth century that it came to the foreground again.[13] There was a renewed commitment to examining the inner life and differing ways of understanding the self. The rediscovery of the self caused the confessional and penitential system to be more introspective,[14] it also brought about the return of the genre of autobiography[15] and the rise of portraiture in art, for example.[16] But it was especially present in theological, spiritual literature. For example, Bernard of Clairvaux, preaching to Cistercian monks on the steps of confession, explained that the first step was expressed in the well-known Delphic precept: "Human being, know yourself." This self-knowledge, writes Bernard, has three elements to it: "that people know what they have done, what they have deserved, and what they have lost."[17] Similarly, when offering advice to Pope Eugenius III, who was also a Cistercian, Bernard told the pope, "Now in order to achieve the fruit of consideration, I think you should consider four things in this order: yourself, what is below you, around you and above you. Your consideration should begin with yourself so you do not reach out to other things in vain,

13. See Morris, *The Discovery of the Individual 1050–1200*; and Sutherland, "The Autonomous Self."

14. See Biller, "Confession in the Middle Ages: Introduction."

15. For example, Archambault, trans. *A Monk's Confession*.

16. Johnson, *Renaissance Art*, 61–75.

17. Bernard of Clairvaux, *Sermones de diversis* 40.3; Griggs, trans. *Bernard of Clairvaux: Monastic Sermons*, 203.

because you have neglected yourself.... Therefore, let your consideration begin and end with yourself."[18] Bernard's Cistercian confrere Aelred of Rievaulx even asked, "How great is man's knowledge when he does not even grasp himself?"[19] And there is perhaps no greater high medieval proponent of self-knowledge than Dante Alighieri (d. 1321), who says that the one who hopes to see God in paradise must "turn and see your own familiar shores" before ascending to God.[20] But knowing oneself is not about self-realization, much less tapping into one's inner self to unlock one's own native spirituality.

No, this inner knowledge is of the Augustinian kind; that is, it is in knowing oneself that makes it possible for one to know God.[21] Even in pagan Gnosticism, self-knowledge was an essential element of "spirituality":

> By awakening to knowledge the gnostic knows reality as it really is: the Fullness as it proceeds from the Unknowable. It is to this Fullness of the true All that the gnostic returns. When the gnostic makes contact with the Light deposited in his soul and totally identifies with it [i.e., self-knowledge], he is back at the place he came from: the Father who is himself the place of repose from which all the worlds (times and spaces) have emanated. There everything finds rest.[22]

---

18. Bernard of Clairvaux, *On Consideration* 2.3.6–2.4.7, Saïd, trans., *Sermons on Conversion*, 52–4

19. Aelred of Rievaulx, *Mirror of Charity* 1.5; Connor, trans., *Aelred of Rievaulx: Mirror of Charity*, 95.

20. Dante Alighieri, *Paradisio* 2.4–5; Esolen, trans., *Dante: Paradise*, 13.

21. See chapter 4 above.

22. Waaijman, *Spirituality*, 336.

The Ongoing Relevance of Thomas' Spirituality

In this understanding, "spirituality" is an awakening that begins within oneself to unlock the "knowledge" (*gnosis*) that lies within. Christian spirituality, on the other hand, begins with self-knowledge for the purpose of getting outside of oneself and back to God. God is not within the human person in this gnostic sense but outside the human person. Self-knowledge and interiority serve the greater purpose of helping the devout follower move outside herself (*exitus* = exit) in order to return (*reditus*) to God.[23] It is God who makes it possible for the believer to love for he is the efficient and final cause. All things come from God as Creator and Savior, and all that exits is made to return. Creation returns in its praise of God, and humans return in union with God in eternal blessedness. Thus, the inner, subjective turn in Christian spirituality is ultimately a return to God, not a deep dive into one's inner being that then becomes the fount of all "spirituality."

At the same time, God makes himself available through the institutional church, primarily by means of the sacraments of baptism and the Holy Eucharist as means of grace. According to Cyprian of Carthage (d. 258), "there is no salvation outside the Church."[24] The context of this epistle concerns the baptism of heretics, with Cyprian holding the position that heretics who were baptized in their heretical "churches" by heretical clergy should present themselves again for baptism once they come into the orthodox Christian church. So, the original context of the quotation concerns salvation but it also addresses a theology of the church as a means of grace.

---

23. See McMahon, *Understanding the Medieval Meditative Ascent*, 1–63.

24. Cyprian of Carthage, *Ep.* 73.21.2; Clarke, trans., *The Letters of St. Cyprian of Carthage, Volume IV*, 66.

That there is no salvation outside the church is built on two theological principles: 1) the one church was established by Jesus Christ; and 2) it is through the church that the graces won by Christ are given to his followers. The Roman Catholic Church states it this way:

> Basing itself upon Sacred Scripture and Tradition, it [i.e., the council] teaches that the Church, now sojourning on earth as an exile, is necessary for salvation. Christ, present to us in His Body, which is the Church, is the one Mediator and the unique way of salvation. In explicit terms He Himself affirmed the necessity of faith and baptism and thereby affirmed also the necessity of the Church, for through baptism as through a door men [sic] enter the Church. Whosoever, therefore, knowing that the Catholic Church was made necessary by Christ, would refuse to enter or to remain in it, could not be saved.[25]

Such a theological conviction leads Anglican theologian Rowan Williams to write, "the Church is most truly itself when it is engaged in sacramental worship; that when above all it meets for the Eucharist, it exists simply as it should and expresses its deepest identity." And, "the Church is supremely the Church when . . . it stands under the Word of God and exposes itself to the act of God in the sacrament."[26] Williams continues to point out that the church is not just fully the church during the event of the Holy Eucharist but at all times:

> the sacramental life of the Church in the narrower sense of the performance of the sacraments, especially the Eucharist, is not to be thought of as an arena of purity and clarity where God is

25. Vatican II, *Lumen gentium* §14.
26. Williams, "The Church as Sacrament," 118.

at work in contrast to the daily existence of the Christian community, with all its unevenness and ambiguity. The Church is a mystery *as a whole*: not only in its praying and feeding but in its vulnerable historical actuality.[27]

The Eucharist connects ordinary humanity with the "sacramental transparency" of the Eucharist so that the communicant and the Church as the People of God are made right with God. The Church's failures are reoriented to the central act of salvation—the cross of Christ: "Its sacramental character is in its confession that it participates in a humanity still in process of enlightenment and transfiguration, still absorbing the effect of the divine act in Christ."[28]

The church, then, as the primary arena for the sacraments (especially baptism and the Holy Eucharist), is the means of grace par excellence. The sacraments themselves are means of grace, but apart from the church there are no sacraments, since the sacraments, according to the *Catechism of the Catholic Church*, for example, "are actions of the Holy Spirit at work in his Body, the Church" (§1116). Likewise, the church is "the faithful steward of God's mysteries" (§1117).[29] In other words, apart from the church there are no sacraments and if there are no sacraments then there is no salvation, much less any notion of Christian spirituality. A devout believer cannot be spiritual but not religious since the one implies and encompasses the other.

The *Imitation* in particular drives this point home by adopting an Augustinian interiority while at the same time explicitly commenting on the necessity of frequent Eucharistic reception (cf. 3.10). Moreover, Thomas stresses

27. Williams, "The Church as Sacrament," 119.

28. Williams, "The Church as Sacrament," 119.

29. Available online at https://www.vatican.va/archive/ENG0015/_INDEX.HTM; accessed May 11, 2020.

the importance of the institution of the church, though indirectly, when he speaks of the dignity of the "office of priesthood": "Oh, how high and honourable is the office of priests, to whom is given power to consecrate with sacred words the Lord of majesty, to bless Him with their lips, to hold Him in their hands, to receive Him in their mouths, and to communicate Him to others" (3.11; 206). Without the institutional church there would be no priests; without priests there would be no sacraments; and without sacraments there would be no salvation. The *Imitation* reminds us that we are not only spiritual, in the full Christian sense of the word, but that we are also devout members of the institutional church. The *Imitation*'s ongoing relevance surmounts the superficiality of the spiritual-but-not-religious mindset, showing it to be neither sufficiently spiritual nor religious.

DISCUSSION QUESTIONS

1. How does the *Imitation of Christ* speak to modern spirituality?
2. What do you think about the concept that "true religion was seated in the heart"?
3. How does Thomas à Kempis' work bridge the gap between personal spirituality and the institution?
4. What is the relationship between knowledge of the self and spirituality?

CONCLUSION

As I said in the "Introduction," this is a book about a book. However, the *Imitation of Christ* is not a book like countless other books. In many ways, it is a "how to" or "owner's" manual. It is not meant to be read and then put on a shelf, but to be *enacted*. It is not just theologizing for theology's sake, but rather seeks to move the believer from one place to another—from childhood to adulthood (to use a biblical image) or from conversion to devotion (to use the language of the Modern Devotion). Historically in the church, images of the spiritual life are not static; that is, they do not think that one merely comes to faith and then does nothing further. No, they depict the spiritual life as a life of movement, growth, and progress. In fact, the motif of the spiritual life as a pilgrimage is common. There is biblical precedent for this image: "Let us go to the house of the Lord!" (Ps 122:1) and Abraham and his descendants "all died in faith, not having received the things promised, but having seen them and greeted them from afar, and having acknowledged that they were strangers and exiles on the earth" (Heb. 11:13), for example. Furthermore, the pilgrimage motif is used in well-known and popular treatises of spiritual formation, such as Bonaventure's *The Journey of the Soul into God* (*Itinerarium Mentis in Deum*) and John Bunyan's *Pilgrim's Progress*. Another popular image, somewhat related to the motif of pilgrimage, is that of the ladder. This too has biblical roots: Jacob "dreamed, and behold, there was a ladder set up on the earth, and the top of it reached to heaven" (Gen 28:12). John Climacus' *Ladder of Divine Ascent* and Walter Hilton's *Scale of Perfection* are two important examples from the history of Christian spirituality that adopt the ladder theme.

Though Thomas à Kempis does not adopt an explicit motif that conveys movement, the *Imitation* most certainly assumes that the reader will be moved by it, so much so that they will strive to imitate Jesus. In this way the *Imitation* sits along other spiritual classics as a manual meant to elicit movement and response from its readers. When Augustine of Hippo sat alone in the garden in Milan, on the verge of finally and fully converting to the Christian faith, two books came to his mind: the Sacred Scriptures and the fourth-century *Life of Anthony* by Athanasius of Alexandria. The details of Augustine's conversion are well known.[1] He hears "a voice from the nearby house chanting . . . saying and repeating over and over again 'Pick up and read, pick up and read.'" Deciding that this voice had no human origin, Augustine interpreted it as a "divine command . . . to open the book [i.e., the Bible] and read the first chapter I might find."[2] But he does this in imitation of Anthony, who, upon walking into church, heard a reading from Matt 19:21: "If you would be perfect, go, sell what you possess and give to

1. See also chapter 2 above.

2. Augustine of Hippo, *Confessions* 8.12.29; Chadwick, trans., *Saint Augustine: Confessions*, 152–53.

Conclusion

the poor, and you will have treasure in heaven; and come, follow me." Anthony's response was to take the text literally, so he sold all he had and became a monk. Augustine followed suit, randomly (or, perhaps, providentially) opening his Bible to Rom 13:13–14: "Let us walk properly as in the daytime, not in orgies and drunkenness, not in sexual immorality and sensuality, not in quarreling and jealousy. But put on the Lord Jesus Christ, and make no provision for the flesh, to gratify its desires." Like Anthony, Augustine responded immediately, by becoming celibate and no longer seeking worldly success. In short, between the Scriptures and the *Life of Anthony* Augustine was moved to move, he was moved to convert. And that is the *telos* of Thomas' *Imitation*. It seeks to move us to convert, to become devout followers of Jesus Christ. Thus, to this end, let us take up and read, take up and read.

DISCUSSION QUESTIONS

1. How does imitation move someone from conversion to devotion?
2. Why is the transformation of the reader a necessary part of the *Imitation of Christ*?
3. How does imitation free us to "move to move"?

Appendix

TRANSLATION OF "THE LIFE OF THOMAS À KEMPIS, CANON REGULAR" BY ANONYMOUS

THE 1494 EDITION OF Thomas' works include an anonymous biography of Thomas.[1] It is assumed that the biography was written by a confrere from Windesheim, especially since it begins with the indication *Auctore incerto penè ccaevo* ("Author anonymous, but almost contemporary"). As Kettlewell notes, not only was the author of the *vita* a contemporary of Thomas but he "had gathered together several things concerning him from his conversation with the Brethren of Mount St Agnes . . . where à Kempis lived

---

1. Thomas Hemerken à Kempis, *Opera et libri vite*.

till he was very old."[2] The life is republished in later editions of Thomas' works but, to my knowledge, has never been translated into English.

THE LIFE OF THOMAS À KEMPIS, CANON REGULAR

Author anonymous, but almost contemporary
Translated by Matthew J. J. Hoskin

THOMAS'S SURNAME WAS HÄMERLEIN, that is, Hammer. He truly was a hammer in his speeches and treatises, for the devout as well as for the undevout, by stimulating the devout through his treatises and by striking their hearts to greater devotion, progress in virtue, and thanksgiving. On the other hand, he was a hammer for the undevout, namely by stirring up their hearts to compunction and examination of their own weakness and imperfection, besides urging them to correction of life; by consoling and strengthening the tested and afflicted; and by showing the way of beginning, progressing, and perfecting in all matters, so that that saying would be rightly written of him now: *They educate many, like the stars in everlasting eternity* (Dan 12:3).[3]

This good and devoted father was very friendly and consolatory to the infirm and tested and extremely zealous for the salvation of people's souls. He desired that they would become saved just as he was himself: thus, in his writings and warnings, instructions and whatever way he could, he would try to draw others with him to the kingdom

---

2. Kettlewell, *Thomas à Kempis*, 6.

3. The full verse reads, "But they that are learned shall shine as the brightness of the firmament: and they that instruct many to justice, as stars for all eternity." (Douay-Rheims)

Translation of "The Life of Thomas à Kempis, Canon Regular"

of the heavens, just as St. Gregory encourages in a certain homily, *etc.*

Since he began, in his youth, to gather riches, namely the riches of virtue, he was allotted a good name. That saying from Lamentations 3 was fulfilled in him, namely: *He is a blessed man who has carried the yoke of the Lord from his youth: he will sit solitary and be silent because he will raise himself above himself, etc.* (Lam 3:27–28).[4]

That which filled him can be generally observed in his treatises, and especially in the *Soliloquy of the Soul*, which he wrote, where Christ his Spouse speaks with his soul, which is to say, His own spouse. Here it is observed how he was seated solitary and was silent, and was raising himself above himself.[5]

If, while this good father was conversing with the congregation [of the Brothers] or with others, he sensed divine inspiration when his Spouse, that is to say Jesus Christ, wished to speak with His spouse, he was accustomed to humbly seek licence, saying, "Beloved brothers, I must go; Someone is waiting for me in my cell." And the brothers, piously agreeing to his request, were greatly built up. In this way that saying was fulfilled in him: *I shall lead him into solitude, and there I shall speak with him* (Hos 2:14). And Thomas himself said this to the Lord: *Speak, Lord, for your servant is listening* (1 Sam 3:10). What he said then to the Lord, and what they said to each other, we have in his treatise, *On the Internal Speaking of Christ to the Faithful Soul*,

---

4. This is literally what the text has here, whereas the Vulgate, Thomas' version of the Bible, has, ". . . because he has lifted [it] upon himself."

5. The text as printed seems corrupt here, giving *lucebat* ("was shining") instead of *tacebat* ("was silent"), and *super sit* instead of *super se*. If emended as I suggest, it provides a parallel with the Scripture verse quoted above. Otherwise it does not make sense.

145

Which His Servant Heard.[6] This treatise has this, in fact, for the theme in its second chapter: *Speak, Lord, for your servant is listening.* This is what the prophet Samuel said to the Lord when the Lord had called him, *etc.*

I have likewise heard many other things about his life and way of living from the brothers of his congregation[7] who are still alive, of which I have narrated scarcely a one-thousandth part in writing this. But what else shall I say? Just as he taught and instructed others by speaking and writing, so also he did by living; by deed he fulfilled what he said ought to be done in his words.[8]

This Thomas à Kempis, having the surname Hammer, was born in the city by the name of Kempen, in the diocese of Cologne. He studied in Deventer in the house of the Brothers, that is to say of the clerics, and was clever, teachable, and affable. As a result, he was very beloved by Dom Florentius and his brothers. Afterwards, when he had been called by God through divine inspiration to the service of the living God, he assented swiftly to divine inspiration, so that the Lord might not reproach him: *I called, and you refused* (Prov 1:24), and so that that saying might not pollute him: *You will call me in your prayers, but I will not hear you, because you refused to listen to my voice.*[9] But Thomas à Kempis did as it is written about St. Andrew—as

---

6. The *Imitation of Christ* III.1 has this chapter heading and III.2 uses the same verse from 1 Samuel.

7. Literally *conventus*, in the sense of an assembly or community. From *convenire*, to assemble/come together.

8. Literally *sermo*, but used in a non-technical sense since it can mean "conversation" or "remarks" as well as formal speeches. It is well-known that Thomas preached, but the parallelism of *opus* and *sermo* here indicates it is broader than preaching.

9. The *vita* cites this as Proverbs 1, but it does not correspond with a specific verse in the Latin Bible.

Translation of "The Life of Thomas à Kempis, Canon Regular"

soon as he heard the voice of the Lord calling him,[10] leaving everything which is of this world, he entered the order of canons regular, which at the time had been recently reformed, namely into the house on Mount St Agnes near Zwolle, in the Year of the Lord 1400. He was invested in the same place in 1406 and so he was proved for six years before he was invested, because at the time it was the custom for people to be proved before being invested, just like gold in a furnace; so gold was tested: *Because he was not proved and tested, what sort of things does he know?*[11] And since he was accepted by God, so it was necessary that with many trials, efforts, and humiliations he would be proved, so that afterwards he would know how to give others the remedy, just as he had often experienced it in himself and others. He also did this in his sermons and treatises.

Thomas progressed greatly in virtue, progressing from day to day, always adding fervor to fervor, devotion to devotion, virtue to virtue, with the result that everyone wondered at his fervor and devotion. And since he was very humble, he deserved to have from God a great and unique grace, as was laid open from his sayings.

Moreover, twice he was subprior, and once procurator. Because he was very inward-focussed and devout, and, therefore, simple in temporal affairs, he was removed from the office of procurator and chosen again for subprior. This was because he bore more fruit by speaking, contemplating, and pursuing prayers. The brothers, thinking over this fact, had mercy on themselves by relieving him from outside business.

In the year of the Lord 1471, the devout Father Thomas à Kempis died, and thus he had served the Lord in the

---

10. See Matt 4:18–20 for the calling of the apostle Andrew.
11. See Sirach 31:10.

APPENDIX

order of canons regular for seventy years in great austerity of life and zealousness of spirit.

And because he wrote and dictated many treatises in his life, and few people know how they are titled, I intend to give titles and write a table of his treatises and books here, so that everyone who reads or hears can know how many there are.

BIBLIOGRAPHY

Allen, Rosamund S., trans. and ed. *Richard Rolle: The English Writings*. London: SPCK, 1989.

Ampe, Albert. *L'Imitation de Jésus-Christ et son auteur*. Rome: Edizioni di Storia et Letteratura, 1973.

Archambault, Paul J., trans. *A Monk's Confession: The Memoirs of Guibert of Nogent*. University Park, PA: Pennsylvania State University Press, 1996.

Arthur, J. P., trans. *The Chronicle of the Canons Regular of Mount St. Agnes*. London: Kegan Paul, Trench, Trübner & Co., 1906.

———. *The Founders of the New Devotion: Being the Lives of Gerard Groote, Florentius Radewin and Their Followers*. London: Kegan Paul, Trench, Trüber & Co., 1905.

Aumann, Jordan. *Spiritual Theology*. London: Sheed and Ward, 1980.

Barron, Caroline, and Nigel Saul, eds. *England and the Low Countries in the Late Middle Ages*. Stroud, UK: Sutton, 1995.

Bauerschmidt, Frederick Christian. *Holy Teaching: Introducing the Summa Theologiae of St. Thomas Aquinas*. Grand Rapids: Brazos, 2005.

Beadle, Richard, and Pamela M. King, eds. *York Mystery Plays: A Selection in Modern Spelling*. Oxford: Oxford University Press, 1984.

Becker, Victor. *L'auteur de l'Imitation et les documents Néerlandais*. La Haye, Netherlands: Nijhoff, 1882.

Bibliography

Bienvenu, Jean-Marc. "Aux origins d'un ordre religieux: Robert d'Arbrissel et la foundation de Fontevraud." *Cahiers d'historie* 20 (1975) 119–35.

Bigg, C., trans. *The Imitation of Christ, Called also the Ecclesiastical Music*. London: Methuen, 1898.

Biggs, B. J. H. *The Imitation of Christ: The First English Translation of the "Imitatio Christi."* Oxford: Oxford University Press for the Early English Text Society, 1997.

Biller, Peter. "Confession in the Middle Ages: Introduction." In *Handling Sin: Confession in the Middle Ages*, edited by Peter Biller and A. J. Minnis, 3–33. York: York Medieval Press, 1998.

Brandsma, Titus. "Twee berijmde Levens van Geert Groote." *Ons geestelijk erf* 16 (1942) 5–51.

Burns, J. Patout. "Grace." In *Augustine through the Centuries: An Encyclopedia*, edited by Allan D. Fitzgerald, 391–98. Grand Rapids: Eerdmans, 1999.

Burton, Janet. *The Monastic Order in Yorkshire 1069–1215*. Cambridge: Cambridge University Press, 1999.

Busch, Johannes. *Chronicon Windeshemense-Liber de Reformatione Monasteriorum*. Edited by Karl Grube. Halle: Hendel, 1886.

Carpenter, James A. *Nature and Grace: Toward an Integral Perspective*. New York: Crossroad, 1988.

Cary, Phillip. "Interiority." In *Augustine through the Centuries: An Encyclopedia*, edited by Allan D. Fitzgerald, 454–56. Grand Rapids: Eerdmans, 1999.

Chadwick, Henry, trans. *Saint Augustine: Confessions*. Oxford: Oxford University Press, 1991.

Clarke, G. W., trans. *The Letters of St. Cyprian of Carthage, Volume IV: Letters 67–82*. Mahwah, NJ: Newman, 1989.

Claussen, M. A. *The Reform of the Frankish Church: Chrodegang of Metz and the* Regula canonicorum *in the Eighth Century*. Cambridge: Cambridge University Press, 2004.

Colledge, Edmund, and James Walsh, trans. *The Ladder of Monks and Twelve Meditations*. London: Mowbray, 1978.

Connor, Elizabeth, trans. *Aelred of Rievaulx: Mirror of Charity*. Kalamazoo, MI: Cistercian, 1990.

Constable, Giles. *Three Studies in Medieval Religious and Social Thought: The Interpretation of Mary; and Martha, The Ideal of the Imitation of Christ, The Orders of Society*. Cambridge: Cambridge University Press, 1995.

Bibliography

Conway, M. Ambrose, and Robert Walton, trans. *Bernard of Clairvaux, Treatises II: The Steps of Humility and Pride and On Loving God*. Kalamazoo, MI: Cistercian, 1980.

Creasy, William C. *The Imitation of Christ by Thomas à Kempis: A New Reading of the 1441 Latin Autograph Manuscript*. Macon, GA: Mercer University Press, 2007.

Cruise, Francis Richard. *Thomas a Kempis: Notes of a Visit to the Scenes in Which His Life Was Spent, with Some Account of the Examination of His Relics*. London: Kegan Paul, Trench & Co, 1887.

Davidson, Clifford. "Northern Spirituality and the Late Medieval Drama of York." In *The Spirituality of Western Christendom*, edited by E. Rozanne Elder, 125–51. Kalamazoo, MI: Cistercian, 1976.

"De origine monasterii Viridisvallis una cum vitis B. Joannis Rusbrochii, Primi Prioris hujus monasterii et aliquot coætaneorum ejus." *Analecta Bollandiana* 4 (1885) 257–308.

Duffy, Eamon. *The Stripping of the Altars: Traditional Religion in England c. 1400–c. 1580*. New Haven, CT: Yale University Press, 1992.

Dumbar, Gerhardi, *Reipublicæ daventriensi ab actis: Analecta, seu Vetera aliquot scripta inedita, Tomus Primus*. Deventer, Netherlands: Johannem van Wyk, 1719.

Dyson, R. W., trans. *Augustine: The City of God against the Pagans*. Cambridge: Cambridge University Press, 1998.

Elm, Kasper. "Die Brüderschaft vom gemeinsamen Leben: Eine geistliche Lebensform zwischen Kloster und Welt, Mittelalter und Neuzeit." *Ons geestelijk erf* 59 (1985) 470–96.

———. "*Vita regularis sine regula*: Bedeutung, Rechtsstellung and Selbstverständnis des mittelalterlichen und frühneuzeitlichen Semireligiosentums." In *Häresie und vorzeitige Reformation im Spätmittelalter*, edited by František Šmahel, 239–70. Munich: Oldenbourg, 1998.

Esolen, Anthony. *Dante: Paradise*. New York: Modern Library, 2004.

Fairweather, A. M., trans. *Nature and Grace: Selections from the Summa Theologica of Thomas Aquinas*. Philadelphia: Westminster, 1954.

Finn, Richard. *Asceticism in the Graeco-Roman World*. Cambridge: Cambridge University Press, 2009.

Forcén, Fernando Espi, and Carlos Espi Forcén. "*Ars Moriendi*: Coping with death in the Late Middle Ages." *Palliative and Supportive Care* 14 (2016) 553–60.

Fry, Timothy, ed. *RB 1980: The Rule of St. Benedict in Latin and English with Notes*. Collegeville, MN: Liturgical, 1981.

Golding, Brian. *Gilbert of Sempringham and the Gilbertine Order c. 1130–c. 1300*. Oxford: Clarendon, 1995.

Goudriaan, Koen. *Piety in Practice and Print: Essays on the Late Medieval Religious Landscape*, edited by Anna Dlabačová and Ad Tervoort. Hilversum, Netherlands: Uitgeverij Verloren, 2016.

Green, R. P. H., trans. *Saint Augustine: On Christian Teaching*. Oxford: Oxford University Press, 1997.

Griggs, Daniel, trans. *Bernard of Clairvaux: Monastic Sermons*. Collegeville, MN: Cistercian, 2016.

Grube, Karl. *Johannes Busch, Augustinerpropst zu Hildesheim: eine katholischer Reformator des 15. Jahrhunderts*. Freiburg im Breisgau: Herder, 1881.

Gründler, Otto. "*Devotio moderna atque antiqua*. The Modern Devotion and Carthusian Spirituality." In *The Spirituality of Western Christendom, Volume 2: The Roots of the Modern Christian Tradition*, edited by Rozanne Elder, 27–45 and 300–303. Kalamazoo, MI: Cistercian, 1984.

Grundmann, Herbert. *Religious Movements in the Middle Ages: The Historical Links between Heresy, the Mendicant Orders, and the Women's Religious Movement in the Twelfth and Thirteenth Century with the Historical Foundations of German Mysticism*. Translated by Steven Rowan. Notre Dame, IN: University of Notre Dame Press, 1995.

Hart, Mother Columba, trans. *Hadewijch: The Complete Works*. London: SPCK, 1980.

Hellinga, Wytze. "Thomas à Kempis—The First Printed Editions." *Quaerendo* 4 (1974) 3–30.

Hendrikman, A. J. et al., eds. *Windesheim 1395–1995. Kloosters, teksten, invloeden. Voordrachten gehouden tijdens het internationale congres '600 jaar Kapittel van Windesheim', 27 mei 1995 te Zwolle*. Nijmegen, Netherlands: Centrum voor Middeleeuwse Studies, Katholieke universiteit, 1996.

Hieromonk Patapios. "*Sub utraque specie*: The Arguments of John Hus and Jacoubek of Stříbro in Defence of Giving Communion to the Laity under Both Kinds." *Journal of Theological Studies* NS 53 (2002) 503–22.

Hill, Edmund, trans. *Essential Sermons*. Hyde Park, NY: New City, 2007.

Bibliography

———. *On Genesis: On Genesis: A Refutation of the Manichees, Unfinished Literal Commentary on Genesis, The Literal Meaning of Genesis*. Hyde Park, NY: New City, 2002.

Hodapp, William F. "Richard Rolle's Passion Meditations in the Context of His English Epistles: Imitatio Christi and the Three Degrees of Love." *Mystics Quarterly* 20 (1994) 96–104.

Hogg, James. "Carthusian Spirituality." In *Analecta Cartusiana* 225, edited by James Hogg, Alain Girard and Daniel Blévec, 27–123. Salzburg: Institut für Anglistik und Amerikanistik, 2005.

———. "The English Charterhouses and the Devotio Moderna." In *Historia et Spiritualis Cartusiensis: Colloqui Quarti Internationalis Acta*, edited by J. de Grauwe, 257–268. Destellenbergen, Belgium: De Grauwe, 1982.

Hoskier, H. C., ed. *De contemptu mundi: A Bitter Satirical Poem of 3000 Lines upon the Morals of the XIIth Century*. London: Bernard Quaritch, 1929.

Huijben, Jacques, and Pierre Debongnie. *L'auteur ou les auteurs de l'Imitation*. Louvain: Bibliothèque de l'Université, Bureaux de la Revue, 1957.

Huizinga, Johan. *The Autumn of the Middle Ages*. Translated by Rodney J. Payton and Ulrich Mammitzsch. Chicago: University of Chicago Press, 1996.

Johnson, Geraldine A. *Renaissance Art: A Very Short Introduction*. Oxford: Oxford University Press, 2005.

Kerns, Brian, trans. *Gregory the Great: Moral Reflections on the Book of Job, Volume 4: Books 17–22*. Collegeville, MN: Cistercian/Liturgical, 2017.

Kettlewell, Samuel. *Thomas à Kempis and the Brothers of the Common Life*. London: Kegan Paul, Trench, & Co., 1885.

Kollmann, Bernd. "Windesheim Congregation." In *Religion Past & Present: Encyclopedia of Theology and Religion, Volume XIII: Tol–Zyg*, edited by Hans Dieter Betz et al., 499–500. Leiden: Brill, 2013.

Kramer, Susan R. *Sin, Interiority, and Selfhood in the Twelfth-Century West*. Toronto: Pontifical Institute of Mediaeval Studies, 2015.

Laetus, Joannes. *Belgii confœderati respublica: seu Gelriæ, Holland., Zeland., Traject., Fris., Transisal., Groning., chorographica politcaque descriptio*. Leiden: Ex officina Elzeviriana, 1630.

Laird, Martin. "Augustinian Spirituality." In *The Bloomsbury Guide to Christian Spirituality*, edited by Peter Tyler and Richard Woods, 57–67. London: Bloomsbury, 2012.

Bibliography

Lawless, George. *Augustine of Hippo and His Monastic Rule*. Oxford: Clarendon, 1987.

Lawrence, C. H. *Medieval Monasticism*. 3rd ed. Harlow, UK: Longman, 2001.

Lekai, Louis J. *The Cistercians: Ideals and Reality*. Kent, OH: Kent State University Press, 1977.

Lerner, Robert. *The Heresy of the Free Spirit in the Later Middle Ages*. Princeton: Princeton University Press, 1972.

Little, Lester K. *Religious Poverty and the Profit Economy in Medieval Europe*. Ithaca, NY: Cornell University Press, 1978.

Louviot, Manon. "Controlling Space, Disciplining Voice: The Congregation of Windesheim and Fifteenth-Century Monastic Reform in Northern Germany and the Low Countries." PhD diss., Universiteit Utrecht, 2019.

Lovatt, Roger. "The Imitation of Christ in Late Medieval England." *Transactions of the Royal Historical Society* 18 (1968) 97–121.

Magill, R. Jay. "Turn Away the World: How a Curious Fifteenth-Century Spiritual Guidebook Shaped the Contours of the Reformation and Taught Readers to Turn Inward." *Christianity & Literature* 67 (2017) 34–49.

Mann, Jill. "Review of Ronald E. Pepin, *Scorn for the World: Bernard of Cluny's "De Contemptu mundi." The Latin Text with English Translation and an Introduction*." *Journal of Medieval Latin* 4 (1994) 163–69.

Martin, Dennis D., trans. *Carthusian Spirituality: The Writings of Hugh of Balma and Guigo de Ponte*. Mahwah, NJ: Paulist, 1997.

McMahon, Robert. *Understanding the Medieval Meditative Ascent: Augustine, Anselm, Boethius and Dante*. Washington, DC: Catholic University of America Press, 2006.

Meade, Denis. "From Turmoil to Solidarity: The Emergence of the Vallumbrosan Monastic Congregation." *American Benedictine Review* 19.3 (1968) 323–57.

Menzies, Lucy. *The Revelations of Mechtild of Magdeburg (1210–1297) or The Flowing Light of the Godhead*. London: Longmans, Green and Co., 1953.

Mercier, J. "Thomas a Kempis." In *Dictionnaire de Théologie catholique, Tome Quinzième, Première Partie: Tabaraud—Trincarella*, edited by A. Vacant et al., 761–65. Paris: Librairie Letouzey et Ané, 1946.

Morris, Colin. *The Discovery of the Individual 1050–1200*. Toronto: University of Toronto Press, 1987.

Bibliography

Mulder-Bakker, Anneke B., ed. *Living Saints of the Thirteenth Century: The Lives of Yvette, anchoress of Huy; Juliana of Cornillon, author of the Corpus Christi Feast; and Margaret the Lame, anchoress of Magdeburg.* Turnhout: Brepols, 2011.

Murk-Jansen, Saskia. *Brides in the Desert: The Spirituality of the Beguines.* London: Darton, Longman and Todd, 1998.

Mursell, Gordon. *English Spirituality: From Earliest Times to 1700.* London: SPCK, 2001.

Mynors, R. A. B., and D. F. S. Thomson, trans. *The Correspondence of Erasmus: Letters 446 to 593, 1516 to 1517.* Toronto: University of Toronto Press, 1977.

Newhauser, Richard. *The Early History of Greed: The Sin of Avarice in Early Medieval Thought and Literature.* Cambridge: Cambridge University Press, 2000.

O'Donovan, Oliver. *The Problem of Self-Love in St. Augustine.* New Haven, CT: Yale University Press, 1980.

Osborne, Jr., Thomas M. *Love of Self and Love of God in Thirteenth-Century Ethics.* Notre Dame, IN: University of Notre Dame Press, 2005.

Outler, Albert C., ed. *The Works of John Wesley.* Nashville: Abingdon, 1984.

Pantin, W. A. "Instructions for a Devout and Literate Layman." In *Medieval Learning and Literature: Essays Presented to Richard William Hunt*, edited by J. J. G. Alexander and M. T. Gibson, 398–422. Oxford: Clarendon, 1976.

Payne, John, trans. *The Imitation of Christ; in Three Books: By Thomas à Kempis.* New York: Collins, 1844.

Penco, Gregorio. *Storia del monachesimo in Italia dalle origine alla fine del Medio Evo.* Rome: Edizioni Paoline, 1961.

Peters, Greg. "Evagrius of Pontus (c. 346–399)." In *Dictionary of Christian Spirituality*, edited by Glen G. Scorgie, 434–35. Grand Rapids: Zondervan Academic, 2010.

———. "Historical Theology and Spiritual Formation: A Call." *Journal of Spiritual Formation and Soul Care* 7.2 (2014) 203–9.

———. *The Monkhood of All Believers: The Monastic Foundation of Christian Spirituality.* Grand Rapids: Baker Academic, 2018.

———. *The Story of Monasticism: Retrieving an Ancient Tradition for Contemporary Spirituality.* Grand Rapids: Baker Academic, 2015.

Peters, Greg, and C. Colt Anderson, eds. *A Companion to Priesthood and Holy Orders in the Middle Ages.* Leiden: Brill, 2015.

Bibliography

Pohl, Michael Joseph. *Thomae Hemerken a Kempis: Opera Omnia, Volume 4*. Freiburg: Herder, 1918.

Post, R. R. *The Modern Devotion: Confrontation with Reformation and Humanism*. Leiden: Brill, 1968.

Powell, L. F., ed. *The Mirror of the Blessed Lyf of Jesu Christ*. Oxford: Clarendon, 1911.

Preble, Henry, and Samuel Macauley Jackson. "The Scorn of the World: A Poem in Three Books." *American Journal of Theology* 10 (1906) 72–101.

Principe, Walter. "Toward Defining Spirituality." *Religion/Sciences Religieuses* 12 (1983) 127–41.

Rapley, Elizabeth. *The Lord as Their Portion: The Story of the Religious Orders and How They Shaped Our World*. Grand Rapids: Eerdmans, 2011.

Ruelens, Charles. *The Imitation of Christ: Being the Autograph Manuscript of Thomas à Kempis, De Imitatione Christi, Reproduced in Facsimile from the Original Preserved in the Royal Library at Brussels*. London: Elliot Stock, 1885.

Saak, Eric L. *Creating Augustine: Interpreting Augustine and Augustinianism in the Later Middle Ages*. Oxford: Oxford University Press, 2012.

———. *High Way to Heaven: The Augustinian Platform between Reform and Reformation, 1292–1524*. Leiden: Brill, 2002.

Saïd, Marie-Bernard, trans. *Sermons on Conversion: On Conversion, a Sermon to Clerics and Lenten Sermons on the Psalm 'He Who Dwells'*. Kalamazoo, MI: Cistercian, 1981.

Scully, Vincent, trans. *Sermons to the Novices Regular by Thomas à Kempis*. London: Kegan Paul, Trench, Trübner & Co., 1907.

Sheldrake, Philip. "What Is Spirituality?" In *Spirituality and History: Questions of Method and Interpretation*, 32–56. New York: Crossroad, 1991.

Sherley-Price, Leo, trans. *Thomas à Kempis: The Imitation of Christ*. London: Penguin, 1952.

Simons, Walter. *Cities of Ladies: Beguine Communities in the Medieval Low Countries, 1200–1565*. Philadelphia: University of Pennsylvania Press, 2002.

Spitzen, O. A. *Thomas a Kempis als schrijver der Navolging van Christus gehandhaafd*. Utrecht: J. L. Beijers, 1880.

Staubach, Nikolaus. "Thomas à Kempis." In *Religion Past & Present: Encyclopedia of Theology and Religion, Volume 12 (Sif-Tog)*, edited by Hans Dieter Betz et al., 689–90. Leiden: Brill, 2012.

Bibliography

Stewart, Columba. *Cassian the Monk*. New York: Oxford University Press, 1998.

Sutherland, J. D. "The Autonomous Self." *Bulletin of the Menninger Clinic* 57.1 (1993) 3–32.

Swafford, Andrew Dean. *Nature and Grace: A New Approach to Thomistic Ressourcement*. Eugene, OR: Pickwick, 2014.

Swanson, Robert N., trans. *Catholic England: Faith, Religion and Observance before the Reformation*. Manchester: Manchester University Press, 1993.

Tanner, Norman P., ed. *Decrees of the Ecumenical Councils, Volume I: Nicea I to Lateran V*. London: Sheed & Ward, 1990.

Tanquerey, Adolphe. *The Spiritual Life: A Treatise on Ascetical and Mystical Theology*. 2nd ed. Tournai, Belgium: Society of St. John the Evangelist/Desclée & Co., 1930.

Teske, Roland J., trans. *Answer to the Pelagians*. Hyde Park, NY: New City, 1997.

———. *Answer to the Pelagians, IV: To the Monks of Hadrumetum and Provence*. Hyde Park, NY: New City, 1999.

Thebaud, Aug. J. "Who Wrote the 'Imitation of Christ'?" *American Catholic Quarterly Review* 8 (1883) 650–71.

Thomas Hemerken à Kempis. *Opera et libri vite*. Nuremberg: K. Hochfeder, 1494.

———. *Opera Omnia*. Edited by Michael Joseph Pohl. 7 vols. Freiburg im Breisgau: Herder, 1910–22.

Thurman, Robert A. F. "Tibetan Buddhist Perspectives on Asceticism." In *Asceticism*, edited by Vincent L. Wimbush and Richard Valantasis, 108–18. New York: Oxford University Press, 1995.

Tyler, Peter. "Triple Way." In *The New Westminster Dictionary of Christian Spirituality*, edited by Philip Sheldrake, 626–27. Louisville: Westminster John Knox, 2005.

Van den Gheyn, J. *Catalogue des Manuscrits de al Bibliothèque Royale de Belgique, Tome Premier: Écriture sainte et Liturgie*. Brussels: Lamertin, 1901.

Van der Woude, Sape, ed. *Acta capituli Windeshemensis: acta van de kapittelvergaderingen der congregatie van Windesheim*. 's Gravenhage, Netherlands: Nijhoff, 1953.

Van Dijk, Rudolf. "De Structuur van de *Navolging*." In *Nuchtere Mystiek: Navolging van Christus*, Hein Blommestijn et al., 35–50. Kampen, Netherlands: Ten Have, 2006.

———. "'Sprich Du zu mir, Du einziger'—Die Dialoge in *De Imitacione Christi*, eine Erkundung." In *Seeing the Seeker: Explorations in the Discipline of Spirituality—A Festschrift for Kees Waaijman on the*

Bibliography

Occasion of His 65th Birthday, edited by Hein Blommestijn et al., 385–404. Leuven: Peeters, 2008.

Van Engen, John. *Sisters and Brothers of the Common Life: The Devotio Moderna and the World of the Later Middle Ages*. Philadelphia: University of Pennsylvania Press, 2009.

———, trans. *Devotio moderna: Basic Writings*. New York: Paulist, 1988.

Van Geest, Paul. "Order, Desire and Grace. Thomas a Kempis' Indebtedness to St. Augustine." In *Aus dem Winkel in die Welt: Die Bücher des Thomas von Kempen und ihre Schicksale*, edited by Ulrike Bodemann and Nikolaus Stauback, 139–57. New York: Lang, 2006.

Van Zijl, Theodore P. *Gerard Groote, Ascetic and Reformer (1340–1384)*. Washington, DC: Catholic University of America Press, 1963.

Verheijen, Luc. "L'*Enarratio in Psalmum* 132 de saint Augustin et sa conception du monachisme." In *Forma futuri: studi in onore del cardinale Michele Pellegrino*, 806–17. Torino, Italy: Bottega d'Erasmo, 1975.

Vigilucci, Lino. *Camaldoli: A Journey into Its History and Spirituality*. Translated by Peter-Damian Belisle. Trabuco Canyon, CA: Source/Hermitage, 1995.

Von Balthasar, Hans Urs. "The Gospel as Norm and Test of all Spirituality in the Church." In *Spirituality in Church and World*, edited by Christian Duquoc and Claude Geffré, 5–13. New York: Paulist, 1965.

Von Habsburg, Maximilian. *Catholic and Protestant Translations of the* Imitatio Christi, *1425–1650: From Late Medieval Classic to Early Modern Bestseller*. Farnham, UK: Ashgate, 2011.

Waaijman, Kees. *Spirituality: Forms, Foundations, Methods*. Leuven: Peeters, 2002.

Weiler, Anton G. "Word from the Beginning: *Principium* in the *Imitatio Christi* of Thomas à Kempis." In *Seeing the Seeker: Explorations in the Discipline of Spirituality—A Festschrift for Kees Waaijman on the Occasion of His 65th Birthday*, edited by Hein Blommestijn et al., 427–40. Leuven: Peeters, 2008.

Wesley, John. *A Plain Account of Christian Perfection*. Peterborough, UK: Epworth, 1952.

White, Paul. *Jodocus Badius Ascensius: Commentary, Commerce and Print in the Renaissance*. Oxford: Oxford University Press, 2013.

Bibliography

Wickstrom, John B. "Carthusians." In *Encyclopedia of Monasticism, Volume I: A-L*, edited by William M. Johnston, 244–47. Chicago: Fitzroy Dearborn, 2000.

Williams, Rowan. "The Church as Sacrament." *International Journal for the Study of the Christian Church* 11 (2011) 6–12.

Wills, Garry. *Augustine's Confessions: A Biography*. Princeton: Princeton University Press, 2011.

Wright, F. A., and T. A. Sinclair. *A History of Later Latin Literature from the Middle of the Fourth to the End of the Seventeenth Century*. London: Routledge, 1931.

Zumkeller, Adolar. "The Spirituality of the Augustinians." In *Christian Spirituality: High Middle Ages and Reformation*, edited by Jill Raitt, 63–74. New York: Crossroad, 1987.

IMITATION OF CHRIST INDEX

1.1	ix, xi, 65, 77, 79, 112, 129	2.10	95, 114
		2.11	95
1.2	54, 87	2.12	95, 114
1.3	72, 85, 87–88, 96–97		
1.4	88, 97	3.1	80, 116–17, 119
1.5	ix, xi, 97	3.2	117–18
1.6	81	3.3	97, 117–18
1.8	88	3.4	118–19
1.9	88	3.5	119
1.10	81, 88	3.7	119
1.11	81	3.8	120
1.17	64, 90	3.9	120
1.18	81, 89, 115	3.10	118, 121, 137
1.19	88, 90–91	3.11	80, 119, 122
1.20	81, 88–91	3.12	120
1.21	81	3.13	123
1.22	77	3.15	123
1.23	78	3.16	123
1.25	90–91, 101, 112, 115	3.17	123
		3.18	124
2.2	81–82, 84, 86, 88, 93		
2.3	95	4.3	97
2.6	83	4.4	93
2.8	97, 115	4.5	86, 91

4.7	93, 114	4.33	83
4.8	93–94	4.34	97–98
4.9	99, 112	4.40	93, 108
4.11	81, 97	4.42	95
4.12	96	4.43	87
4.13	82, 93, 114	4.47	96
4.14	94	4.48	79
4.15	82, 88, 115	4.49	79–80, 112
4.19	96, 112	4.50	91
4.20	91	4.51	77
4.21	99, 102, 115, 118	4.53	82, 84, 108, 115
4.27	83–85, 98, 115, 130	4.54	110–11
4.28	92	4.55	112
4.31	83, 97–100, 111	4.59	97
4.32	83, 97		

SCRIPTURE INDEX

GENESIS

1	65
1:26–27	80
3:16	82
28:12	140

1 SAMUEL

3:10	145

PSALMS

6:4	38
18:15	38
20:13	27
49:21	27
50:15	39
122:1	139

PROVERBS

1:24	146

LAMENTATIONS

3:27–28	145

DANIEL

12:3	144

HOSEA

2:14	145

SIRACH/ECCLESIASTICUS

31:10	147

MATTHEW

4:18–20	147
5:3	85
6:10	82
11:28	115
15:18–20	90
19:21	140

Scripture Index

22:37–39	84
26:39	23

LUKE

5:16	89
14:26	94

ACTS

2:44–46	2
2:45	62
4:32	2, 12

ROMANS

3:24	102
5:3	95
9:5	38
13:13–14	39, 141

1 CORINTHIANS

10:13	96
13:12	98

EPHESIANS

1:3–10	127
1:9–10	109
2:8–9	102

PHILIPPIANS

2:5–9	92

COLOSSIANS

1:16–17	109

1 TIMOTHY

4:7–8	81

HEBREWS

11:13	140

2 PETER

1:4	118

SUBJECT INDEX

Aelred of Rievaulx, 20, 134
Albigensian heresy, 22
Alexander IV, pope, 6
Alighieri, Dante, 4, 99, 103, 134
Anselm of Canterbury, 14, 21, 117
Antony of Egypt, 39
apatheia, 99
"apostolic life," 21
Arnhem, 21
ars moriendi, 78
asceticism, 12, 80
Athanasius of Alexandria, 2, 80, 93, 140
Atkinson, William, 69
Augustinian Canons, xii, 3, 6, 8–10, 22, 27, 48, 125
Augustinian Canons of the Order of the Holy Cross (Croziers), 53

Beghards, 21–22, 47
Beguines, 21–25, 31, 47
Bernard degli Uberti, 5

Bernard of Clairvaux, 14, 20, 27, 36–37, 67, 74–75, 86–87, 98–100, 130, 133–134
Bernard of Cluny, 78
Bonaventure, 70, 75–76, 130, 140
Boniface IX, pope, 50
Brinckerinck, John, 48, 52
Brugman, John, 53
Bruno of Cologne, 4–5
Bunyan, John, 140
Busch, Johannes, 29, 43

Camaldoli, 5
Carthusians, 4–5, 19–21, 32, 90
Cassian, John, 2, 74, 77, 83, 90
Chrodegang of Metz, 3, 11–12
Chronicle of the Canons Regular of Mount St. Agnes, 55
Cistercians, 3, 5, 13, 19, 27, 90

Subject Index

Clement of Alexandria, 73–74
Climacus, John, 140
Cloud of Unknowing, 15
collations, 52
Commentary on the Song of Songs, 74
Confessions, 26–27, 37–39, 77, 94–95, 99–100, 102, 118, 140
Confutation of Tyndale's Answer, 69
contemplation, 19–20, 55, 74–75, 107
contemptus mundi, 78
conversio (conversion), 35–40, 43, 139
Corpus Christi, feast, 58, 105–107
Cur Deus Homo, 117
curiosity (*curiositas*), 88, 97
Cyprian of Carthage, 135

Damian, Peter, 11, 92
Dannhäuser, Peter, 59–60
definitores, 13
De contemptu mundi, 78
Deventer, 31–32, 35–36, 44, 45, 51–52, 54, 146
Dier, Rudolph, 9–10, 34–35
Dominicans, 3, 21, 47
domus pauperum (houses for children), 52
donatus, 56–58

Eemsteijn, 10

Ennarrationes in Psalmos (*Running Explanations on the Psalms*), 61
Erasmus of Rotterdam, 44, 52–54
Eugenius III, pope, 133
Evagrius of Pontus, 74
ex opere operato, 104
exercitium (exercise), 36
extranei (students from outside the city), 52

first order, 9, 47
Fontevraud, abbey of, 5
Franciscans, 3, 21, 47
fuga mundi, 65

Gerson, John, 67–70
Gilbert of Sempringham, 5
Gilbertines, 5
Gnostikos, 74
grace, 7, 27, 40–42, 74, 75, 77, 80, 82, 86, 93, 98, 101–26, 130, 135–37, 147
"Great Union," 6
Gregory VII, pope (Hildebrand), 11
Gregory XIII, pope, 30
Gregory the Great, 45, 74
Grote, Geert, 9, 21, 31–37, 40–44, 48–52, 55–56, 61, 67–68
Gualbert, John, 5
Guigo I, 21
Guigo II, 19–20
Guigo de Ponte, 20
Guzzolini, Silvestro, 5

Subject Index

Hadewijch, 24
Henry of Guelders, bishop, 106
Hildesheim Cathedral, 29
Hilton, Walter, 15, 70, 140
Honorius III, pope, 22
humility, xi, 3, 12, 34, 35, 74, 88, 91–95, 120
hypostatic union, 117

Ignatius of Loyola, 76
illumination, 75–76, 91, 103
Innocent IV, pope, 6

Jacques de Vitry, 22
John XXII, pope, 6
Jordan of Quedlinburg, 61, 63, 89
John of the Cross, 76
John the Baptist, 123
Joseph II, emperor, 30
Julian of Norwich, 15
Juliana of Cornillon, 105

Kephalaia Gnostica, 74

Ladder of Divine Ascent, 140
Ladder of Monks, 19–20
Law, William, 131
Leeder, Clemens, 29–30
Liber Vitasfratrum (Book of the Lives of the Brothers), 61
Life of Anthony, 140–41
Life of Christ, 27
Love, Nicholas, 15, 17
Low Countries, 14, 23
Lower Rhine, 51

Ludolph of Saxony, 27, 67

Marie d'Oignies, 22
Mechthild of Magdeburg, 23–24
meditation, 18–21, 69, 75, 89, 130
Meditations of the Life of Christ, 15, 17, 19
Meditations on the Passion, 18
Michael of Massa, 27
Modern Devotion, xii, 20–21, 23, 29–50, 53–54, 130, 139
Monnikhuizen, 21
More, Thomas, 69
Mt. St. Agnes, Zwolle, 55, 57–58, 61, 68, 106, 125, 143, 147

Napoleon, 4, 30
Nature and Grace, 109–10
Nemelerberg, 55
Neo-Platonists, 26
Nicene-Constantinopolitan Creed, 117

Olivetan reform, 5
On Contemplation, 20
On Matrimony, 33–34
Order of the Hermits of St. Augustine (OESA), 6, 25
Origen of Alexandria, 73–74

Pantaléon, Jacques, archdeacon, 106
Paris, University of, 31, 68
patience, 24, 91, 93, 95–96

Subject Index

Pelagius, 109,
perfection, 61, 62, 74–75, 84, 98–100, 131–32
Peter Lombard, 103
Pilgrim's Progress, 140
Plain Account of Christian Perfection, 131–32
Pomerius, Henry, 43
Praktikos, 74
Pirkamer, George, 59
prudence, 6, 91, 96–98
Pseudo-Anselm, 130
(Pseudo-)Bonaventure, 67
Pseudo-Dionysius the Areopagite, 75–76
purgation, 75–78, 91

Radewijns, Florentius (Florens), 9, 35–36, 51, 54
reading, xi, 12, 19–20, 39, 52, 60, 62, 73, 103, 130–132
Reformation, 4, 30, 53, 55, 76, 124
resolutio/intentio (resolution/intention), 31, 35–36, 39–43
Robert of Arbrissel, 5
Robert of Molesme, 5
Robert of Thourotte, bishop, 105
Rolle, Richard, 15, 18
Romuald of Ravenna, 5
Rule of Augustine, 3, 6, 12–13, 40, 46, 50
Rule of Benedict, 3, 11, 46, 88
Rule for Canons, 11
Ruusbroec, John, 43

saeculum, 64
Santa Sabina, 16
Scutte, John Oude, 33
second order, 47
self-denial, 78, 80–83, 88, 96
self-love, 81, 83–87, 94
self-knowledge, 87, 133–35
Scale of Perfection, 70, 140
Sermons to the Brothers in the Desert, 6–8
Silvestrines, 5
simony, 32
Simplicianus, 8
Sisters and Brothers of the Common Life, xii, 21, 29–50, 61, 62, 131
socii (companions), 34
spirituales (spirituals), 34
"spiritual but not religious," 127–28, 137–38
St. Martin, Liège, 106
St. Peter's, Utrecht, 35
Steps of Humility and Pride, 74
Suso, Henry, 130

Taylor, Jeremy, 131
Teresa of Avila, 76
tertiaries, 47
The Journey of the Soul into God, 140
The Life of the Good Monk, 59, 64
The Mirror of the Blessed Life of Jesus Christ, 15
The Triple Way, 75
third order, 47–49

Subject Index

Thomas Aquinas, 88, 92, 96, 104–5, 121–22
Tolomei, Bernard, 5
Transiturus de hoc mundo, 106
"triple way," 74–76

Urban IV, pope, 106

Valerius, bishop, 7–8
Vallombrosa, 5
Veneranda sanctorum, 6
Virgin Mary, 75, 123
visitores, 13

Von Baden, Frederic, bishop, 53

Wesley, John, 131–32
William of St-Thierry, 14, 27
Windesheim Congregation, xii, 9–13, 21, 29–30, 48, 50, 59, 68, 106

York Minster, 16

Zerbolt, Gerard, 37, 41–42, 52
Zwolle, 10, 52, 55–56, 58, 68, 106, 147

www.ingramcontent.com/pod-product-compliance
Lightning Source LLC
Chambersburg PA
CBHW020851160426
43192CB00007B/880